The Counselor's Helpdesk

Phil Travers

FAMILY VIOLENCE PREVENTION SERVICES, INC.

BROOKS/COLE

THOMSON LEARNING

Australia • Canada • Mexico • Singapore • Spain • United Kingdom • United States

BROOKS/COLE

THOMSON LEARNING

Executive Acquisitions Editor: *Lisa Gebo*
Assistant Editor: *Alma Dea Michelena*
Marketing Team: *Caroline Concilla, Tami Strang, Megan Hansen*
Editorial Assistant: *Sheila Walsh*
Project Coordinator: *Laurel Jackson*
Production Service: *Buuji, Inc.*

Manuscript Editor: *Alan DeNiro*
Permissions Editor: *Sue Ewing*
Cover Design: *Roy R. Neuhaus*
Cover Photos: *Photodisc*
Print Buyer: *Jessica Reed*
Typesetting: *Buuji, Inc.*
Printing and Binding: *Webcom Ltd.*

For more information about this or any other Brooks/Cole product, contact:
BROOKS/COLE
511 Forest Lodge Road
Pacific Grove, CA 93950 USA
www.brookscole.com
1-800-423-0563 (Thomson Learning Academic Resource Center)

For permission to use material from this work, contact us by
www.thomsonrights.com
fax: 1-800-730-2215
phone: 1-800-730-2214

Printed in Canada

10 9 8 7 6 5 4 3 2

Library of Congress Cataloging-in-Publication Data
Travers, Phil.
    The counselor's helpdesk / Phil Travers.
        p. cm.
    Includes bibliographical references and index.
    ISBN 0-534-52633-0 (alk. paper)
        1. Counseling. 2. Counseling—Study and teaching.   I. Title.

BF637.C6 T67 2001   2001035337
361'.06—dc21

TCNJ BOOKSTORE 609-637-5000

4150 CASH-1   6929 0759 008

9780534452633 NEW
TRAVERS/COUNSELOR'   MDS 1N   45.65
                    TOTAL   45.65

ACCOUNT NUMBER   5200XXXXXXXXXXX
   Visa/Mastercard   45.65
Expiration Date   08/06
   Authorization   005706

LAST DAY FOR TEXTBOOK RETURNS 9-7-04

                     9/02/04 7:14 PM

ALL OTHER MERCHANDISE WITH A RECEIPT:
- Get a FULL REFUND anytime in your original form of payment
- Software must be unopened for exchange or refund (Open software may be exchanged for the identical item only)

WITHOUT A RECEIPT:
- Merchandise credit will be given at the current selling price
- Cash back on merchandise credits will not exceed $10

NO REFUNDS GIVEN:
- On textbooks after 30 days from the start of class
- On textbooks without a receipt
- On custom course materials, outlines, study guides, magazines, and prepaid phone cards

Textbooks and all other merchandise must be in saleable condition.

SAVE THIS RECEIPT

REFUND POLICY

TEXTBOOKS WITH A RECEIPT:
- FULL REFUND within first week of class
- After first week of class, get a FULL REFUND within 2 days of purchase
- After second day of purchase, get a 75% refund
- Summer or special course session REFUNDS accepted for ONE WEEK ONLY after start of class

ALL OTHER MERCHANDISE WITH A RECEIPT:
- Get a FULL REFUND anytime in your original form of payment
- Software must be unopened for exchange or refund (Open software may be exchanged for the identical item only)

WITHOUT A RECEIPT:
- Merchandise credit will be given at the current

In ainm an Athar agus an Mhic agus an spioraid Naoimh. Amen.
In the name of the Father, and of the Son, and of the Holy Spirit. Amen.

About the Author

Phil Travers is a Licensed Professional Counselor with Family Violence Prevention Services, Inc. Phil has counseling experience in the domestic violence, sexual assault, and sexual identity fields. He earned his Master of Arts and Educational Specialist degrees in community counseling from James Madison University in 1998. To contact Phil, please send e-mail to ptravers@stic.net, or visit him online at www.mylifechanges-sa.com.

Phil and Gil, his partner, live in San Antonio, Texas, with their children—Ben, age 17, and Sam, age 14—and their dog, James.

Contents

PART THREE

Alphabetical Index of Selected Theories 55

PART FOUR

Useful Forms and Phone Numbers 69

Index 95

Preface

Welcome to *The Counselor's Helpdesk*, a resource guide designed to help you become the best counselor you can be as you navigate through the often complex world of ethical, effective counseling. I wrote this book for advanced counselor interns, counselors, their educators, and clinical supervisors. It is also for experienced counselors seeking a handy resource for frequently needed information. Social workers, caseworkers, psychologists, and psychiatrists will likely find this information helpful, too. I use the word *counselor* to refer to any professional change agent. Students in their first practicum experience are encouraged to use a text for beginning students as a supplement to this book.

The Counselor's Helpdesk was born out of my in-the-field experiences. As a recent graduate of a CACREP-approved counselor education program, when I began my internship, I found many helpful people but little concise, reliable, practical information to help me help my clients; the same may be true at your internship site.

Counselor education programs do an incredibly good job of preparing us for working with clients. Our internship sites help us develop and refine our skills so we can be more effective. Our clients help us realize the gaps in our experiences when they ask for information we cannot readily provide.

The Counselor's Helpdesk is divided into four parts: (1) an Alphabetical Index of Client Issues, (2) an Alphabetical Index of Counselor Information, (3) an Alphabetical Index of Selected Theories, and (4) Useful Forms and Phone Numbers. A wide range of information about the practice of counseling is presented in a concise, easy-to-read-and-use format. This book is designed for *active use* during sessions, phone calls, supervision, consultation, and charting. Although *The Counselor's Helpdesk* is designed to assist you in your work as a counselor, *it does not replace seeking supervision and/or consultation*, nor is it a substitute for any school, agency, or licensing board guidelines. Rather, *The Counselor's Helpdesk* is a supplement to the assistance already available to you. I hope you will find it a handy reference.

In Part 1, the Alphabetical Index of Client Issues, each topic includes the following subcategories: Important Considerations, Intervention, Documentation, Ethical Considerations, and Further Reading. Where appropriate, Part 1 topics also include the section Signs and Symptoms. Part 2, the Alphabetical Index of Counselor Information, contains suggestions for practicing professionally. Topics in Part 2 also include suggestions for further reading. In Part 3, the Alphabetical Index of Selected Theories, you will find a brief review of several classical counseling approaches, with each topic including the theory's foundation and techniques, as well as reading suggestions. In Part 4, Useful Forms and Phone Numbers, you will find a wide variety of commonly needed forms and telephone numbers that will help you help your clients.

I've kept the information concise because, for the advanced intern, you are near the end of your graduate training. The material here is intended to refresh your memory of the many training experiences you had in graduate school. Counselor educators and clinical supervisors will also find this book useful in aiding the intern's development as a professional counselor. As a practicing counselor, the format of *The Counselor's Helpdesk* will appeal to you, too. Counseling is a challenging, demanding, fast-paced career; here you will find the information you need to be a better helper.

Some information you will not find here—for example, detailed descriptions of challenges clients may face, long explanations of theories, information about the licensure process, specifics of insurance billing, tips on finding employment, and so on. There are many other books that address those concerns. *The Counselor's Helpdesk* is designed to help you with the actual work you do with clients.

I want to hear from you about this book—what you found helpful, what you'd like to see added or changed, and any other comments or questions you might have. Please send your correspondence to me in care of Brooks/Cole.

Acknowledgments

To Gil, Ben, and Sam: I don't think "thank you" will ever convey how much your support and love during this project meant to me. I love each of you dearly.

Love, kindness, and compassion are three words that so beautifully describe my mother. Mom, I thank you for your help and support with this project.

A heartfelt thank-you to Maria Monte and Kathy Ruiz for refreshing my spirit. You are God's hands in action.

The late Dr. Dan Daniel continues to have a profound impact on my life and my work as a counselor. My experiences with him helped shape my approach to counseling. Dan was one of those rare individuals with the gift for being himself in any situation. Dan, you are missed.

Dr. William O. Hall, Jr., believed in me. Thank you, Bill, for teaching me so much about life, being a counselor, and being a professional. I would not be the person I am today without your mentoring, wisdom, and kindness.

I also wish to thank my reviewers—Stephen Felt, Idaho State University; Dona Kennealley, University of South Dakota; Jackie Leibsohn, Seattle University; Chad Mosher; and Geoffrey Yager, University of Cincinnati—for their professionalism and assistance in improving this book.

Finally, thank you to my friends at Brooks/Cole for their guidance, advice, support, and belief in this project.

Phil Travers

▼▼▼

Alphabetical Index
of Client Issues

Part 1 reviews frequently encountered client issues, presenting problems, and client concerns. Remember to seek supervision and consultation as necessary.

Aging

Important Considerations

- Aging is an inescapable reality of life. As children, growing older is an exciting adventure. As a young adult matures, she or he experiences new freedoms and responsibilities. For older adults, aging brings a refinement of abilities. As the aging process continues, knowledge can become wisdom.
- Aging brings other changes, too: the loss of a child's excitement and joy, evolving relationships with parents and siblings, the growth of romantic relationships, the birth of children, the death of parents and friends, the loss of abilities, and, indeed, our own death.

Intervention

While aging is a continual process, many people rarely think about their aging until they reach certain milestones (e.g., turning 21, 30, 50, 65, etc.). As a result, some clients may choose to seek counseling for aging-related concerns (e.g., changes in ability, perceived loss of attractiveness) after a milestone-related crisis occurs (e.g., realizing that one is 40 years old). Erikson's stages of development provide a useful approach for helping clients understand their experiences.

Erikson contends that the successful resolution of each stage of development leads to a healthy personality. However, people neither completely resolve, nor completely fail to resolve, any particular developmental stage. Rather, as each stage is encountered, individuals have varying levels of success in resolving that particular crisis. A more successful resolution in one stage leads to more successful resolutions in later stages. To refresh your memory, Erikson's stages and the approximate ages in which they are encountered are presented in Figure 1.1.

Counseling is an ideal setting for resolving the conflicts that occur in each of the stages. The theory and approach you choose will depend upon your client's needs and your preferences.

Documentation

You may wish to document in the casenote (a) the stage of development the client is currently in, (b) her or his attempts to resolve the associated struggle, and (c) any difficulties that occurred in the previous stages. This information will help you understand the client and develop an effective treatment plan.

Ethical Considerations

While helping clients resolve developmental challenges from their earlier years, some clients may recall episodes of abuse. When this occurs, you should seek supervision and consultation for information about how to best help your client (see **Child Abuse and Neglect, Consultation, Domestic Violence,** and **Supervision** later in this book).

Integrity Versus Despair (60+)
Generativity Versus Stagnation (40s and 50s)
Intimacy Versus Isolation (20s and 30s)
Identity Versus Role Confusion (Adolescence)
Industry Versus Inferiority (5–12)
Initiative Versus Guilt (3–5)
Autonomy Versus Shame and Doubt (2)
Trust Versus Mistrust (1)

Figure 1.1. Erikson's stages of development. Source: Adapted from *Life-span Development,* Fifth Edition, by J. W. Santrock, pp. 40–41. Copyright © 1995 WCB, Benchmark & Benchmark Publishers. Reproduced with permission of The McGraw-Hill Companies.

Further Reading

Myers, J. E., & Schwiebert, V. L. (1996). *Competencies for gerontological counseling.* Washington, DC: American Counseling Association.

AIDS/HIV

Important Considerations

- AIDS is a human disease. Anyone of any age, ethnicity, sexual orientation, socioeconomic status, or level of education can become infected. Any client could be infected with HIV.
- HIV is the virus that causes AIDS. AIDS is the progressive terminal disease that results from HIV.
- Home tests are now available for HIV testing. These kits contain testing materials and are sent to a facility for analysis. Oral and blood testing is also available from doctor's offices and clinics.
- Although treatments are available for the symptoms of AIDS/HIV infection, they are incredibly expensive.
- All blood drawn for use in hospitals and clinics is tested for HIV and certified safe before transfusion. It is unlikely that a client would have contracted HIV from a blood transfusion after 1985.
- HIV is transmitted through the direct sharing of bodily fluids, typically blood and/or semen, from an infected individual's body to another person's body. Unprotected sex and needle sharing transmit HIV easily.
- There is no cure for AIDS.
- There is no vaccine against HIV.
- In some states, anonymous testing is not available.
- Some states routinely test all blood drawn for HIV.
- A negative (−) test result means a person has not been exposed to HIV in a manner that could infect her or him.
- A positive (+) test result means a person has been exposed to and is infected by HIV. A positive result does not mean a person has developed AIDS.

Intervention

Deciding to be tested for HIV may be an overwhelming process, because many clients wonder what they will do if their test results are positive. They begin to make tentative plans about their life while they await the results. It frequently takes two to three weeks for test results to become available. Some clients are in crisis during this waiting period and may need more counseling sessions to help them process their feelings.

Clients who test negative should be provided with educational information about AIDS. Some clients see a negative result as validation that their behaviors are safe when, in fact, they may be quite risky. Counseling about choices, feelings, and taking care of oneself is also important for the client who tests HIV-negative.

Clients with AIDS or who are HIV-positive need medical care in addition to counseling. If your client is not receiving medical care, you should refer her or him for appropriate treatment (see **Useful Forms and Phone Numbers**). Safety planning is a vital component of counseling those with AIDS or who are HIV-positive.

Group counseling for people with AIDS or who are HIV-positive is helpful because it reduces isolation and provides access to resources. Counseling a client with AIDS may involve funeral planning; finding meaningful ways to say "goodbye"; and working through intense feelings of fear, anxiety, depression, loss, self-hatred, and anger. People with AIDS or HIV experience many losses and may come to counseling with a variety of needs. Many people with AIDS are, for a medley of reasons, cut off from family and friends.

Your client may not have AIDS or be HIV-positive, but someone in her or his family may be. Working with family, friends, and caregivers is just as important. Anticipatory grief, anger, and depression may be present. Education about what AIDS is, how it is spread, and what to expect as the disease progresses may also be appropriate.

Documentation

Recording a client's HIV status can be a perplexing situation, especially if her or his records are available to third parties, such as insurance companies. Even so, you should follow established ethical guidelines for casenotes (see **Casenotes**).

Ethical Considerations

If a client reports unsafe or risky sexual and/or drug-related contact with another person, you may have a duty to warn the other individual of his or her potential for contracting a life-threatening disease. Consult with your supervisor regarding the laws in your state.

Further Reading

Kain, C. D. (1996). *Positive: HIV affirmative counseling.* Washington, DC: American Counseling Association.
Kalichman, S. C. (1996). *Answering your questions about AIDS.* Washington, DC: American Psychological Association.

Anger

Important Considerations

Anger is a powerful and often frightening emotion. It is also a healthy emotion because it alerts us to situations that disturb us. Unexpressed and inappropriately expressed anger can cause a client difficulties. Learning to express anger in appropriate ways is challenging for most people. Many people never learned how to express their anger appropriately. Rather, they may have learned that anger is a key to power over another. For these people, it is easier to "be angry" than it is to express what they are angry about.

Intervention

The first step in helping a client with her or his anger is to discover what he or she has learned about anger. What messages were received from parents about anger? Was anger seen as an emotion to be tucked away, vented explosively, or expressed in a healthy way? Who in the family was "allowed" to be angry? Just Dad? Just Mom? Everyone? No one? What other feelings surround anger? Guilt? Power? Fear?

Explosive expressions of anger are psychologically abusive and may lead to physical and/or sexual abuse. These clients may need to see a counselor who specializes in the treatment of domestic violence (see **Domestic Violence**). Some clients admit they have difficulty with anger and may not realize that they are being abusive. Anger management programs may be appropriate for some clients; violence intervention programs may be more appropriate for others. Anger is abusive when it is expressed inappropriately.

The healthy expression of anger involves honesty. To express anger appropriately, the client must first realize and understand what he or she is angry about. After helping the client develop skills to identify what she or he is angry about, the next step is to help the client develop the communication skills needed to express her or his angry feelings and needs while respecting the rights of others. Reality Therapy (see **Reality Therapy Approach**) and Rational Emotive Therapy (see **Rational Emotive Therapy Approach**) are excellent approaches for helping clients learn to express anger appropriately.

Unless you have specific training in therapeutic techniques to help clients physically express their anger, you should not encourage a client to act out her or his anger because of the possibility of physical harm to the client or to you.

Documentation

In addition to recording the client's progress, you should also record significant themes in the client's anger (e.g., "I'm not good enough," "I'm not safe if I'm not in complete control," etc.). Tracking these themes will assist you in developing a comprehensive treatment plan that could also address other concerns, such as the development of self-esteem and communication skills.

Ethical Considerations

If your client desires a counseling approach that involves the direct, physical expression of anger, you should refer her or him to a counselor trained in such techniques.

Explore with the client how she or he expresses anger at home. If the client is abusive to her or his family, you may need to report the abusive behavior to the appropriate agency in your state (see **Frequently Called Numbers** and **Useful Forms and Phone Numbers**).

If a client is intensely angry during the session and threatens to harm another person, you may need to report this threat to the police department, the sheriff's department, and/or the threatened person (see **Frequently Called Numbers** and **Useful Forms and Phone Numbers**). Consult with your supervisor regarding the laws in your state.

Further Reading

Gentry, W. D. (2000). *Anger free: 10 basic steps to managing your anger.* New York: Quill.

Anxiety

Important Considerations

Anxiety occurs in several different ways; each is debilitating and frequently prevents the client from living a full life. The anxious client may avoid the doctor or dentist in spite of desperately needed medical care. Loneliness may be the result of social phobia. A strained relationship may result from generalized anxiety.

Signs and Symptoms

People suffering from anxiety frequently avoid situations that might trigger it.

Frequently Encountered Types of Anxiety

Generalized anxiety disorder
Panic disorder
Obsessive-compulsive disorder

Posttraumatic stress disorder
Specific phobia
Social phobia

Generalized anxiety disorder: a general sense of uneasiness or fear—lasting over a long period of time—that something, sometime will go wrong.

Posttraumatic stress disorder: long-term, pervasive anxiety resulting from a traumatic event, such as abuse, death of a loved one, war, rape, or natural disasters—characterized by flashbacks and nightmares.

Panic disorder: fear of an event or situation that leads to a dramatic, frightening physical reaction that includes symptoms such as chest pain, embarrassment, sweating, dizziness, and/or heart palpitations.

Specific phobia: fear of a specific object (e.g., bridges, spiders, heights) or event (e.g., going to the dentist, falling).

Obsessive-compulsive disorder: obsessions are thoughts that preoccupy the client; compulsions are behaviors that the client believes will relieve the obsessive thoughts. Compulsive behaviors range from mild (such as gently rubbing the thumb against the forefinger) to severe (such as self-mutilation).

Social phobia: also called "shyness," social phobia prevents the client from interacting with friends, potential friends, or colleagues.

Intervention

Reality Therapy (see **Reality Therapy Approach**), Rational Emotive Therapy (see **Rational Emotive Therapy Approach**), and the Brief/Solution-Focused Approach (see **Brief/Solution-Focused Approach**) are beneficial treatment approaches with most clients who experience anxiety. Systematic desensitization is advantageous, especially with phobias. Supportive group counseling is also helpful for clients experiencing anxiety. Anxiety and depression can co-occur (see **Depression**).

When working with compulsions, it is very helpful to understand how they are related to the obsessions in order to develop a realistic treatment plan.

Asking about the client's previous attempts to resolve her or his anxiety will help you develop a more effective treatment plan.

Many clients experiencing anxiety respond well to the newer tranquilizers and antidepressant medications (e.g., lorazepam, alprazolam, Prozac, Zoloft, Paxil, etc.). Clients may be referred to a family physician or psychiatrist if you and your client feel medication would be helpful. Exercise may also benefit anxious clients.

Documentation

Documenting the client's experience with anxiety during the course of treatment will help you track the client's progress and refine your treatment modality.

Ethical Considerations

To make or recommend a diagnosis, refer to "Anxiety Disorders" in the *DSM-IV-TR* (p. 429).

Further Reading

Ellis, A. (1999). *How to control your anxiety before it controls you.* Secaucus, NJ: Birch Lane Press.

Birth Order/Parenting

Important Considerations

Every child grows up in a different family—even if they have the same mother and father. As each child is born into the family and the parents continue to grow and develop, the family changes into a new and different series of relationships. Even when the parents decide to have no more children, the family continues to grow and develop as children develop and eventually leave the home. Children of families who experience divorce, remarriage, or the death of a sibling or parent also experience dramatic changes in their development.

Attention to birth order is not voodoo. Rather, birth order makes sense as an important variable in the development of personality. There are few set rules to the analysis of birth order. There are characteristics associated with the "first born," "middle born," and "last born." However, the children in any particular family may express first-born characteristics without necessarily having been first born. For example, if the first-born child experiences a severe accident, that child might be treated as the last born, while the middle child might be treated as the first born. A close look at the family constellation points to birth order-related elements of personality development.

Children who assume a first-born role are likely to be leaders and perfectionists (Leman, 1998). Children who assume a middle-born role are likely to be good mediators and act well adjusted to life (Leman, 1998). Children who assume a last-born role are likely to expect that most things will go their way, and they tend to enjoy being in the spotlight (Leman, 1998). Clients who assumed the first-born role may need assistance in learning to relax and to share responsibility and decision making with others. Clients who assumed a last-born role may need assistance in learning to be flexible and to take responsibility. Clients who assumed a middle-born role may need assistance in learning to speak up for their own wishes and needs.

Parenting is important and challenging work. First-, middle-, and last-born children all have different parenting needs. Most parents learn how to parent from their own parents, and although many children learn important and useful parenting techniques, most parents encounter situations for which they are unprepared. *Parenting With Dignity* is the most effective parenting program I have found. The program is focused on skills and information to help parents maintain their dignity and their children's dignity. Thoughtful, thorough, and affordable, *Parenting With Dignity* is available through the Drew Bledsoe Foundation (www.drewbledsoe.com).

Documentation

Using a genogram (see **Genograms**) will help you discover the birth order and its impact on your client.

Ethical Considerations

If a potentially abusive or neglectful situation is reported to you, report it to the appropriate authorities (see **Child Abuse and Neglect**).

Further Reading

Leman, K. (1998). *The new birth order book: Why you are the way you are.* Grand Rapids, MI: Revell.

Boundaries

Important Considerations

- Helping clients with their boundaries requires that you be aware of your own boundaries and that you model appropriate boundaries within the counseling relationship.
- Clients develop rigid or diffuse boundaries to protect themselves from a perceived threat.
- Changing boundaries is challenging, lifelong work.

Intervention

Boundaries separate us from other people in the world. Boundaries begin emerging at birth and continue to develop across the lifespan. The development and maintenance of healthy boundaries occurs best in an environment free of abuse (see **Domestic Violence, Sexual Abuse,** and **Substance Abuse**) where appropriate boundaries are modeled. Boundaries protect us, physically and emotionally, from potential harm. Our boundaries also change during our lifetime. Boundaries such as "Don't talk to strangers," which may be appropriate for a child, are usually very dysfunctional for an adult. Boundary difficulties arise when a client has either no boundaries or very rigid boundaries.

The client with very rigid boundaries prevents anyone from getting close physically or emotionally. This client may never visit the doctor or dentist because the rigid boundaries prevent the doctor from completing an examination. This client may have few friends, frequently experiences great difficulty in trusting anyone—including counselors—and often describes herself or himself as being "surrounded by a wall." The goal with this client is to adjust the boundaries slowly so appropriate interactions can occur (e.g., completing a dental exam, going to a dinner party, etc.).

At the opposite extreme, the client with very diffuse or no boundaries feels out of control, as if her or his life is controlled by others—and often it is. Clients with diffuse boundaries experience extreme difficulty saying no and expressing their own feelings, especially negative feelings. They often allow people they do not like into their lives, consider *everyone* a "dear friend," and describe themselves as "doormats." The goal with this client is to adjust the boundaries slowly so that appropriate interactions can occur (e.g., having time to oneself, expressing a wide range of emotions, etc.).

The presence of rigid boundaries or the absence of any boundaries at all serves a purpose for the client—usually protection from a perceived threat. For a client to make lasting changes to her or his boundaries (i.e., to make them appropriate), the examination of her or his current boundaries and the situations that developed them is critical to change. Reality therapy (see **Reality Therapy Approach**), combined with person-centered counseling (see **Person-Centered Approach**), is an ideal approach for boundary work. The solution-focused approach is also appropriate (see **Brief/Solution-Focused Approach**).

Boundary work is lifelong. Clients who have experienced boundary difficulties in the past will more than likely find themselves revisiting boundary issues as time passes. Encourage your clients to expect this, and share with them that changing boundaries can be very hard work.

Documentation

In addition to other relevant information, record significant events in the development of the client's boundaries and previous attempt at change.

Ethical Considerations

Some clients with boundary difficulties are sexually promiscuous, too. If a client engages in unsafe sexual activity with multiple partners, you may have a duty to warn her or his significant other. Consult with your supervisor.

If a diagnosis is warranted, consult "Antisocial Personality Disorder" or "Borderline Personality Disorder" in the *DSM-IV-TR* (pp. 701, 706).

Further Reading

Black, D. W. (1999). *Bad boys, bad men: Confronting antisocial personality disorder.* New York: Oxford University Press.

Katherine, A. (1991). *Boundaries: Where you end and I begin.* New York: MJF Books.

Career Counseling

Important Considerations

A person's work life affects her or his home life; the reverse is also true. Doing satisfying work increases the potential for a satisfying home life.

Most people work many hours each week, often working several jobs to help "make ends meet." Balancing time at work and time with the family is challenging.

Many people cannot find satisfying work because of a lack of jobs accessible to them, a lack of skills, family members in need of special care, or any combination of these or similar factors. Two considerable barriers to employment include education and transportation.

A frequent challenge for many workers is finding opportunities for meaningful work within their present jobs and opportunities for advancement. Most workers enjoy worthwhile challenges that foster their creativity.

Intervention

Career counseling often begins with the use of inventories or assessments to identify an individual's strengths, interests, abilities, achievements, and aptitudes in order to stimulate the individual to think about a variety of possible careers or general areas of interest (e.g., working with people, building things, working outside, etc.). Although assessments and inventories provide a wide variety of useful information, they cannot be used alone to identify potential careers for the individual.

The counselor must also interview the client about her or his needs, past work experiences, desired work experiences, and goals. The interview provides the counselor with a richer, more detailed picture of who the client is than assessments will alone. Assessments may suggest that a client would be suited to certain types of work, but the client may have other wishes for her or his career future.

Career counseling provides another avenue for helping clients who present other concerns, such as depression or anxiety. For some clients, a career change may relieve other concerns and help them live life more fully. For clients who are not working, completing education or a training program and obtaining a job can be a source of satisfaction and pride.

Career counseling can include activities such as developing and enhancing interview skills, assisting with writing resumes, teaching job research skills, and identifying networking possibilities available to the client.

Documentation

Copies of all assessment reports should be kept in the client's file.

Ethical Considerations

Use only those psychological assessments that you are qualified to use (see **Psychological Assessment**).

Further Reading

Zunker, V. G. (1994). *Career counseling: Applied concepts of life planning* (4th ed.). Pacific Grove, CA: Brooks/Cole.

Child Abuse and Neglect

Important Considerations

- Abuse includes physical, emotional, medical, and sexual acts that cause harm or injury to the child.
- Symptoms of physical abuse include unexplained injuries, frequent "falls," multiple bruises in various stages of healing, and unusual fractures.
- Neglect includes physical, medical, emotional, and educational deprivation that prevents the child from functioning fully.
- Symptoms of neglect include inappropriate clothing for the weather, an untreated medical condition, and a lack of support and love.
- There is no "standard profile" of an abused or neglected child. Children of any age, ethnicity, socioeconomic level, or gender can be abused or neglected by their parents.
- Although cultures define discipline and abuse differently, the laws of your locality define what is reportable to the appropriate authorities.
- A lack of financial resources does not imply abuse or neglect. A parent who cannot provide all the "bells and whistles" for a child is not abusive or neglectful. The basic needs of food, shelter, clothing, safety, medical care, and emotional support must be met. A parent does not have to provide the latest clothing or gourmet food, or live in the best neighborhood.

Intervention

The child's safety is paramount. Abuse and neglect must be reported in a timely manner to the appropriate agency in your locality, usually Child Protective Services (CPS) or the police department. Timely reporting enables CPS to take appropriate action to protect the child from harm. If for any reason you are unable to contact CPS and the child is in grave danger, contact the local police department or children's shelter (see **Frequently Called Numbers**) for assistance.

In many localities, Child Protective Services cannot investigate every report of child abuse and neglect. Often there are too many reports and too few investigators to research them. If you feel the child is in a highly dangerous situation, be certain to make that clear in your report. Because of the limitations of CPS, it is important that you develop a list of alternative services. A list of parenting classes provided by reputable agencies may be helpful. A referral to an agency that provides intensive in-home counseling/parenting services is also useful, as well as a list of competent family counselors.

Even if you are fairly certain that CPS will not investigate your report of child abuse and/or neglect, you must make your report. This is important for several reasons. First, you are ethically (and in many states legally) required to do so. Second, you do not know if there are other reports about a family on file with CPS. Your report may be the one that provides impetus for an investigation or an offer of services. Third, do not underestimate the effect of abuse and neglect. A child who is well dressed and has "good grades" might be abused or neglected at home.

Documentation

Record any abuse the client reports in as much detail as possible without interrogating the client. When reporting child abuse to a state agency, state your name and the name of the agency from which you are calling. Record the information-taker's name in the client's file along with the date and time you called, length of the call, and the information you discussed (see **Report of Information**).

Ethical Considerations

It is not for you to decide if Child Protective Services will investigate a report of child abuse. If a client reports any abuse or neglect of a child, it must be reported to the appropriate agency in your locality.

If your client is unable or unwilling to report child abuse, you are required to do so. Contact your local CPS office to make the report (see **Frequently Called Numbers**). If your client chooses to make the report, she or he should do so in your presence so you can document that the abuse was reported. In most circumstances, it is advisable to tell the client you will make the report if she or he chooses not to do so.

If you question whether or not a situation may be abuse or neglect, consult your supervisor or another trusted colleague immediately.

If a potentially abusive or neglectful situation is reported to you, report it to the appropriate authorities.

Further Reading

Helfer, M. E., Kempe, R. S., Krugman, R. D., & Kempe, R. S. (Eds.). (1999). *The battered child.* Chicago: University of Chicago Press.

▼▼▼
Death and Dying

Important Considerations

Kübler-Ross conceptualizes the dying person progressing through these stages in an orderly fashion. I envision clients cycling through each stage in no particular order, and revisiting the stages as death approaches. See Figure 1.2:

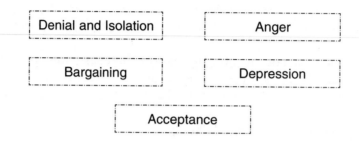

Figure 1.2. Kübler-Ross's stages. Source: Adapted from *Life-span Development*, Fifth Edition, by J. W. Santrock, p. 583. Copyright © 1995 WCB, Benchmark & Benchmark Publishers. Reproduced with permission of The McGraw-Hill Companies.

Intervention

There are several groups of people you may work with related to this topic: people who are dying, family and friends of people who are dying, and others who work with those who are dying (e.g., doctors, nurses, etc.). Although the needs of these groups are different, they have much in common, too. Feelings of loss, guilt, and confusion are emotions that unite these groups.

The dying individual's reaction to her or his impending death varies based on her or his experiences. Children may be frightened and often lack an understanding of what death is. Young adults may feel cheated and angry. Older adults may feel a rush to complete their goals. Very old adults may welcome death as a relief from pain or loneliness. Many dying people are scared of death—especially the process of dying. Dying people may wonder how their body will be cared for after death, if dying will hurt, if heaven or hell is in their future, how their children and/or spouse will care for themselves, and so on. Dying clients who seek counseling often seek help with the process of dying. This process can involve fulfilling unmet goals, resolving feelings, learning about death, or exploring religious and spiritual concerns.

For the family and friends of the dying person, a wide variety of reactions often occur. Many are frightened and may wonder who will tuck them in at night when mommy dies, will daddy come back, what will life be like after my parents die, what will life be like without my friend, how will I manage this house without my spouse, what will my identity be without my spouse, and so on. Some clients may even feel relief, especially if the dying person is experiencing extreme pain or has been abusive to the family. These clients often seek counseling for help with their feelings, fears, and thoughts about death.

For caregivers such as doctors, nurses, and in-home helpers, death may be seen as a clinical event. However, many caregivers are saddened when a patient dies, especially if the caregiver feels they did not "do enough," made some mistake that he or she feels caused the patient's death, or if they knew the dying person for an extended period of time. Caregivers may wonder if they will ever "get it right," what their colleagues will think of them, if this line of work is "right" for them, or what the "value" of life is.

Helping these clients involves helping them with their concerns and feelings about death and dying. An educational approach combined with person-centered counseling (see **Person-Centered Approach**) is often most helpful.

Documentation

Record the client's affect, progress, and goals.

Ethical Considerations

It is important that you consider your own thoughts, feelings, and beliefs about death and dying.

If the client's pending death or recent death is causing disruptions in your life, consult your supervisor and seek counseling as necessary.

Further Reading

Turner, M. (1998). *Talking with children and young people about death and dying: A workbook*. Philadelphia: Brunner-Routledge.

Depression

Important Considerations

Although depression is a commonly encountered concern, it should not also be considered a trivial one. When a client reaches out for help, this may the first, only, or last time they are willing to take this risk. Ask about depression, explore previous experiences with depression, evaluate coping mechanisms, and never let the call for help be answered by an echo. See Figure 1.3 for frequently encountered types of depression.

Signs and Symptoms

- Loss of interest in usually enjoyable activities
- Significant weight gain or loss
- Increased or decreased sleep
- General sense of exhaustion
- Difficulty concentrating and making decisions
- Low self-worth, feelings of guilt, or low self-esteem
- Sadness, frequent crying
- Thoughts of suicide

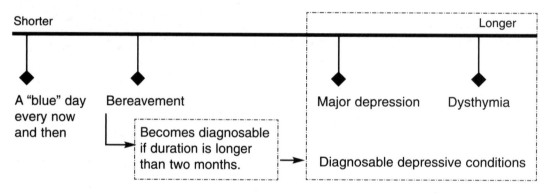

Figure 1.3. Frequently encountered types of depression.

Bereavement: An extended period of grief after the death of a parent, child, spouse, or friend, an accident, or other traumatic event.
Major depression: A period of significantly depressed mood (see **Signs and Symptoms**) lasting at least two weeks.
Dysthymia: Mild-to-moderate depressed mood (see **Signs and Symptoms**) lasting at least two years. Major depression can co-occur with dysthymia.

Intervention

Depression, regardless of cause or duration, is an intensely painful, often life-stopping event. Although many depressed clients continue to function (e.g., go to work or school, raise a family, etc.) they frequently feel a deep emptiness inside and that they are not "living." The hopelessness associated with depression makes changing feelings, thoughts, and behaviors challenging. Depression and anxiety can co-occur (see **Anxiety**). Charting patterns of feelings, thoughts, and behaviors in the depression will help guide treatment planning.

Reality therapy (see **Reality Therapy Approach**), rational emotive therapy (see **Rational Emotive Therapy Approach**), and the brief/solution-focused approach (see **Brief/Solution-Focused Approach**) are beneficial treatment approaches with most depressed clients. Supportive group counseling is also helpful.

Many clients experiencing depression respond well to the newer antidepressant medications (e.g., Prozac, Zoloft, Paxil, etc.). Clients may be referred to a family physician or psychiatrist if you and your client feel medication would be helpful. Exercise has also been shown to benefit depressed clients.

Documentation

In addition to any referrals you make, record your assessment of suicidality and affect after each session.

Ethical Considerations

To make or recommend a diagnosis, refer to "Mood Disorders" in the *DSM-IV-TR* (p. 345). Evaluate depressed clients for suicidality (see **Suicide** and **Suicide Assessment Checklist**).

Further Reading

Shafii, M., & Shafii, S. L. (Eds.). (1992). *Clinical guide to depression in children and adolescents*. Washington, DC: American Psychiatric Press.

Beckham, E., & Leber, W. R. (Eds.). (1995). *Handbook of depression*. New York: Guilford Press.

Divorce

Important Considerations

Divorce happens with great regularity and affects everyone in the family, not just Mom and Dad. Divorce brings dramatic emotional and financial changes.

Intervention

Divorcing couples who have children would do well to attend a class designed to help them help their children with the divorce process. Children in divorcing families have special needs that need to be met regardless of how the parents feel about each other. Children need to know that they are loved, that they will be cared for, and that their parents are still their parents, even if they are no longer married and no longer live in the same house. Spouses should avoid putting their children "in the middle" at all costs. Groups such as Parents Without Partners may also be helpful.

The spouses have special counseling needs too. Many spouses, even if they wanted the divorce, are saddened by the loss of the relationship, are unsure how to proceed with future relationships, have financial concerns, and question their self-worth. Some spouses lose their identity when the marriage ends. Some spouses have safety concerns as well—their ex-spouse may stalk them.

An amicable divorce is best for all involved. However, having an amicable divorce can be extremely difficult when feelings of bitterness, guilt, and jealousy contaminate the process. Boundary work (see **Boundaries**) may be appropriate. Communication skills may also need to be developed or enhanced.

Little is known about the divorce process experienced by gay and lesbian couples. While gay and lesbian people cannot legally marry, some of their relationships do end, and when they end the spouses are confronted with many of the same concerns as their heterosexual counterparts. Gay and lesbian people often experience additional difficulties. When other family members do not know about the relationship, they cannot offer comfort and support to the gay or lesbian person (see **Gay and Lesbian Concerns**).

Documentation

You should document all referrals you make (e.g., divorce classes, parenting classes, etc.) in the client's file. If a client reports that her or his ex-partner is stalking her or him, you should document this as well.

Ethical Considerations

It is unethical to persuade clients to stay married or to divorce. For clients thinking about divorce, your job is to help them with the decision-making process.

Further Reading

Sommers-Flanagan, R., Elander, C., & Sommers-Flanagan, J. (2000). *Don't divorce us*. Washington, DC: American Counseling Association.

Domestic Violence

Important Considerations

- Any one can be a victim/survivor or a batterer, regardless of socioeconomic background, religious affiliation, occupation, education, age, ethnicity, or sexual orientation.
- Types of domestic abuse include: physical, verbal, psychological, and sexual abuse. A victim may experience one of these, all, or any combination.
- Safety planning is critical, especially when counseling victim/survivors. The victim/survivor decides what is appropriate because she (and sometimes he) is the only person who knows and understands how dangerous the relationship is.
- Learning new behaviors such as communication skills, appropriate interpersonal boundaries, methods of improving self-esteem, and the appropriate expression and management of feelings are helpful to both victim/survivors and batterers.
- Assisting clients experiencing domestic violence in accessing resources may help reduce stress (e.g., financial problems, etc.) and decrease the likelihood of further violence.

Intervention

Physical abuse includes shaking, punching, restraining, and slapping. Verbal abuse includes putdowns, name calling, threatening, and screaming. Psychological abuse includes a batterer's efforts to confuse the victim, destroying treasured possessions, threatening to hurt the children, intimidation, and coercion. Sexual abuse is any unwanted sexual activity. Frequently these abuses co-occur, with verbal and psychological abuse occurring apparently more frequently than physical or sexual abuse. While physical or sexual abuse may appear more dramatic than verbal or psychological abuse, verbal and psychological abuse can typically occur on a daily basis.

For victims, education about the nature of domestic violence and safety planning is vital. Because of the dynamics of domestic violence, many victims are unaware that what they are experiencing is violence. Creating a safety plan is critical. Help the client develop a concrete plan (e.g., "Where will you stay?" or "How can you reduce the number of weapons in your home—such as kitchen knives?"). Future counseling will likely include the development of appropriate interpersonal boundaries (see **Boundaries**) and a healthy self-esteem.

For batterers, education about what domestic violence is and learning new behaviors are vital. Many batterers want to change their behavior but do not know how to make changes. Creating specific alternative behaviors, such as taking a time out, talking about feelings, and acknowledging fears, is critical to changing behavior. Future counseling will likely include the development of appropriate interpersonal boundaries (see **Boundaries**) and a healthy self-esteem. Group counseling is often very helpful to batterers.

Many victims and batterers were sexually abused as children. For safety reasons, couples or family counseling is not recommended until after the batterer and victim(s) have received individual counseling, developed a safety plan, and had access to community resources.

Many victims and batterers will need access to legal help, medical care, career counseling, and financial assistance. Victims may also need emergency shelter.

Documentation

Documentation should include any reported injuries (body location, description, and reported cause). Pictures should be taken as well by an appropriate staff member. A witness should also be present when photographs are taken. Record your assessment, evaluation, intervention, and referrals in the client's file (see **Casenotes**).

Ethical Considerations

If the client reports child abuse to you, you must report the abuse to the appropriate agency in your state.

Further Reading

Wilson, K. J. (1997). *When violence begins at home: A comprehensive guide to understanding and ending domestic abuse.* Alameda, CA: Hunter House.

Dreams

Important Considerations

The interpretation of dreams is perhaps ultimately best left to the dreamer. Some dreams have significance and deep meaning; other dreams probably do not. As you will recall, Freud believed that dreams were the "royal road to the unconscious"—that dreams assisted in making conscious the unconscious. From a Freudian point of view, nearly all dream symbols possess sexual meaning. Jung also theorized extensively about dreams. Jung, like Freud, believed that dreams provide access to unconscious material. However, unlike Freud, Jung did not believe that dream symbols had sexual content.

Most clients remember dreams backwards, describing the end first (Ackroyd, 1993). Everyone dreams; however, not everyone may remember her or his dreams or the full content of the dreams. Clients who wish to explore their dreams may find it beneficial to keep a tablet or tape recorder next to their bed to facilitate recording dream details. Taking a few moments to relax in bed before starting the day may encourage the remembering of dreams.

When clients approach you with dreams, they want to share, listen to them, and when asked, encourage them to draw their own conclusions, interpretations, and meanings. People interpret their dreams accurately and seek assurance that their interpretation is "right" or accurate. The dreamer is the only person with the full context of her or his life and is the only one who can decide what the dream means.

Documentation

Document discussing dreams in the casenote and the client's interpretation of the dreams. Avoid focusing on specific details of the dreams, which may be used out of context if the client goes to court.

Ethical Considerations

If a client decides that a dream means she or he must harm herself or himself or another, you should report this danger to the appropriate agencies and people. Consult with your supervisor regarding the laws in your state.

Further Reading

Ackroyd, E. (1993). *A dictionary of dream symbols: With an introduction to dream psychology.* London: Blanford Press.

Freud, Sigmund. (1950). *The interpretation of dreams* (A. A. Brill, Trans.). New York: Modern Library.

Hall, J. A. (1983). *Jungian dream interpretation: A handbook of theory and practice.* Toronto: University of Toronto Press.

Eating Disorders

Important Considerations

- Eating disorders of adolescence and adulthood include anorexia nervosa and bulimia nervosa.
- Feeding and eating disorders of infancy and early childhood include pica, rumination disorder, and feeding disorder.
- Anorexia and bulimia may be expressions of control by a family member who cannot gain control over her or his life in any other way. Anorexia and bulimia occur primarily in women.
- All eating disorders can be fatal.

Intervention

Systems approaches (see **Systems Approaches**) and behavioral approaches (see **Behavioral Approach**) are commonly used in the treatment of eating disorders. Systems approaches are used to treat the family. The member with the eating disorder is frequently the "identified patient." The eating disorder is rarely "the problem"; rather, it is a symptom of problems within the family system. From this perspective, changes in the family system will be necessary to promote behavioral change within the identified patient.

People experiencing anorexia maintain an extremely low body weight, rarely eat, and when they do eat, they do not eat appropriately. The weight loss associated with anorexia is seen by the client as a success and not as a problem, making the treatment of anorexia very difficult.

People experiencing bulimia maintain a normal body weight, eat excessively huge quantities of food, and then purge the body of the consumed food through the use of laxatives, diuretics, and/or vomiting. Food is used to "stuff" feelings, and the purging, used to relieve guilt, may also produce a "buzz" or "high."

Documentation

Document all referrals you make (e.g., to a physician), and check with the referral to verify the client is seeking treatment at that location.

Ethical Considerations

To make or recommend a diagnosis, refer to "Eating Disorders" in the *DSM-IV-TR* (p. 583), or "Feeding and Eating Disorders of Infancy or Early Childhood" in the *DSM-IV-TR* (p. 107).

The treatment of eating disorders requires specialized training and resources. Do not attempt to treat a severe eating disorder unless you have specialized training and supervision.

Further Reading

Claude-Pierre, P. (1999). *The secret language of eating disorders: How you can understand and work to cure anorexia and bulimia.* New York: Vintage Books.

▼▼▼
Gay and Lesbian Concerns

Important Considerations

- The only way you can tell if someone is gay or lesbian is if she or he tells you. There is no definitive look, signal, or occupation that means a person is gay or lesbian. Your office can be a safe place if you are comfortably open to the possibility that any client may be gay or lesbian.
- For some gay and lesbian clients, concerns about their sexual orientation will be their primary reason for seeking counseling. For many it will not be. Do not assume that a client's sexual orientation is their reason for coming to counseling. Be sure to ask your client about her or his counseling needs.
- Many gay and lesbian teens are at a higher risk of suicide than their heterosexual peers.
- There is no evidence to suggest that reparative therapies are successful or benefit the client.
- Several counselor characteristics may prevent effective counseling of gay and lesbian clients. Among these characteristics are: unresolved sexual orientation, homophobia, religious values, lack of contact with or knowledge of the gay and lesbian community, and ignorance of AIDS and HIV, among others.

Intervention

Counseling gay and lesbian clients is very similar to counseling other clients. A focus of accepting oneself "as is" is very appropriate, because there is growing evidence that being gay or lesbian has a highly biological component. The more comfortable you are with yourself, the easier it will be for gay and lesbian clients to be comfortable with you. Knowledge combined with good counseling skills are effective tools for helping your gay and lesbian clients.

"Coming out," the process in which the individual begins to publicly acknowledge her or his sexual identity, is one of the hardest things a person can do at any age. Fundamentally, coming out is a developmental challenge like none other because our society assumes everyone to be heterosexual. Sexual orientation is not a visible characteristic. In spite of the challenges coming out presents, it is also one of the most important components in the development of a healthy gay or lesbian life. Imagine not being able to share your life with the people most important to you (e.g., family, friends, and co-workers). Gay and lesbian clients who remain "in the closet" commonly feel guilt, shame, doubt, and anxiety. All these emotions make it difficult for the gay or lesbian person to function and add powerful stresses to gay and lesbian relationships.

Gay and lesbian people in rural areas may be especially isolated because few gay and lesbian community groups may exist. Additionally, there may be few or no gay and lesbian role models. This can be especially devastating to teenagers who may feel as if they are "the only one." Isolation can lead to a sense of desperation that leads some gay and lesbian persons to make poor relationship choices.

For gay and lesbian clients in relationships, a wide variety of patterns exist. Some gay and lesbian persons were previously in heterosexual relationships and already have children. Some gay and lesbian couples adopt children. Others may use artificial insemination. Some gay and lesbian couples do not have children. Many gay and lesbian couples are of mixed ethnic heritages. The modern family no longer (if it ever did) resembles *Father*

Knows Best, My Three Sons, or the *Brady Bunch.* Today's families take many forms, and as a counselor, you should be prepared to work with them.

Although AIDS/HIV is a human disease rather than a gay and lesbian disease, you should be prepared to discuss, openly and accurately, how HIV is spread and to help your gay and lesbian clients assess their risk (see **AIDS/HIV**).

Documentation

Some clients (e.g., those in the armed forces) may be very concerned about what you write in their file, especially if their sexual orientation could have a direct impact on their employment. Your casenotes should follow established professional guidelines (see **Casenotes**), and you should explore the client's fears with her or him.

Ethical Considerations

If for any reason you feel you cannot work with a gay or lesbian client, you must refer her or him to a competent mental health professional.

If you feel that you can work with a gay or lesbian client but are unsure of how to proceed, seek consultation with a qualified professional.

Further Reading

Travers, P. (2000). *Counseling the rainbow: Effectively meeting the needs of gay and lesbian clients.* San Antonio, TX: My Life Changes.

Personality Disorders

Important Considerations

- Personality disorders have pervasive effects in the client's life.
- All types are debilitating and frequently prevent the client from living a full life.

What are Clusters?

The *DSM-IV-TR* uses clusters, or dimensional models, to group personality disorders "based on descriptive similarities" (p. 685; see Table 1.1). Refer to *DSM-IV-TR* (p. 689) for descriptions of the dimensional models.

Intervention

Each person's personality develops out of a variety of experiences and environmental influences. However an individual's personality is described, that personality developed for a reason. The child who experiences abuse may well develop a personality disorder as a form of protection or defense. While this personality disorder may serve to protect her or him as a child, the disorder will very likely become problematic in adult life.

Changing personality is a long-term counseling endeavor. Many clients may have neither the time, money, nor interest in changing their personality. However, many treatment options exist. For example, a client who is diagnosed with Avoidant Personality Disorder might be taught skills to help her or him interact with others. The client may dread interacting with people but could develop necessary skills to help facilitate her or his daily life. Reality therapy (see **Reality Therapy Approach**), rational emotive therapy (see **Rational Emotive Therapy Approach**), and the brief/solution-focused approach (see **Brief/Solution-Focused Approach**) are beneficial treatment approaches. Psychoanalysis (see **Psychoanalytic Approach**) may be especially effective in the reconstruction of personality.

Documentation

Personality disorders are recorded on Axis II (see **DSM-IV-TR Use**), *DSM-IV-TR*, pp. 27–34.

Table 1.1 *DSM-IV-TR* Personality Disorders

Type	Cluster	Type	Cluster
Antisocial personality disorder	B	Narcissistic personality disorder	B
Avoidant personality disorder	C	Obsessive-compulsive personality disorder	C
Borderline personality disorder	B	Schizoid personality disorder	A
Dependent personality disorder	C	Schizotypal personality disorder	A
Histrionic personality disorder	B	Personality disorder not otherwise specified	N/A
Paranoid personality disorder	A		

Ethical Considerations

While all diagnoses should be made carefully and with great consideration, this is especially true in the case of the personality disorders. Personality disorders are considered long-lasting, pervasive, and difficult to treat.

To make or recommend a diagnosis, refer to "Personality Disorders" in the *DSM-IV-TR* (p. 685).

Further Reading

Stone, M. H. (1993). *Abnormalities of personality: Within and beyond the realm of treatment.* New York: Norton.

Sexual Abuse

Important Considerations

- Some people who were sexually abused have no memory of the events; these are often called repressed memories. There is much debate over the validity of repressed memories.
- Sexual abuse can be physical (touching, intercourse, etc.) or nonphysical (exposure), and often involves physical abuse (punching, restraining, etc.) and psychological abuse (threats, secrecy, etc.).
- Anyone of any age could be sexually abused.
- Sexual abuse does not determine sexual orientation.
- Nearly all people who were sexually abused experience lasting effects of the abuse (e.g., nightmares, depression, feeling "dirty," rage, etc.).
- Anyone could be a sexual abuser. Frequently, sexual abusers know their victim and gradually build up to the abuse.
- A child may have been sexually abused if she or he
  a. avoids the alleged perpetrator or is seductive and/or anxious in that person's presence (Haugaard & Reppucci, 1988).
  b. cycles through admitting being abused and retracting the claim (Haugaard & Repucci, 1988).
  c. experiences genital pain, infection, and/or bleeding (Telep, 1991).
  d. displays age-inappropriate sexual knowledge and/or behavior (Telep, 1991).

Intervention

If a client reveals sexual abuse, it is vital that you do not overreact to her or his disclosure—*be calm.* Overreaction stifles the client's ability to express herself or himself. If you overreact, you may likely be seen by the client as unhelpful and unprofessional. As you might imagine, being sexually abused is a horrific experience—do not make it any more difficult for your client. Remain calm and let the client share her or his experiences with you at her or his own pace.

Active listening, expression of feelings, and safety planning are critical. Avoid asking questions. If you feel the need to ask the client questions it is important that you ask questions that respect the client's struggle. Avoid judgmental questions, such as "Didn't you try to get away?" or "How come you didn't tell an adult?" Appropriate questions could include "Do you need medical attention?" "How are you taking care of yourself?" and so on. If you ask too many questions, you begin to sound like others who may have attempted to help your client (e.g., police officers, detectives, doctors, etc.)

Although there is frequently much debate about the validity of claims of sexual abuse, especially those claims made years after the abuse occurred, accept what your client shares with you. A client who reports sexual abuse was most likely sexually abused. The dynamics of sexual abuse (e.g., secrecy, pain, guilt, threats, etc.) may prevent a client from accepting the reality of the abuse she or he experienced until years after the abuse occurred. Sexual abuse by a family member often has more severe and lasting effects than sexual abuse by a stranger.

Documentation

Recent sexual abuse should be documented in detail, in the event that the client chooses to pursue legal action against the alleged perpetrator.

If a child reports sexual abuse, carefully document the client's report to assist you in making your report to Child Protective Services.

Ethical Considerations

You must report the current sexual abuse or suspected sexual abuse of children to Child Protective Services.

Sexually abused clients should receive medical attention if they were physically hurt or had physical contact with the alleged perpetrator or her or his bodily fluids.

Further Reading

Dale, P. (1999). *Adults abused as children: Experiences of counseling and psychotherapy.* Thousand Oaks, CA: Sage.

Nyman, A., Svensson, B., & Barnen, R. (1997). *Boys: Sexual abuse and treatment.* Bristol, PA: Jessica Kingsley Publishers.

Substance Abuse

Important Considerations

- Substance abuse is common, and all clients should be screened for such abusive behaviors.
- Clients who are actively abusing substances will not be able to make meaningful changes until they have addressed their substance abuse issues.

Intervention

Alcohol is a commonly used drug, and the context of its use helps to determine if abuse is occurring; for example, when alcohol is used to escape problems, avoid feelings, or avoid meaningful human interactions, or when the use of alcohol causes significant problems in a client's life. Some of these problems might include missing work or school due to drinking, needing more and more alcohol to achieve the same effect, and needing a drink to be "social." Health problems of long-term alcohol abuse include permanent and fatal liver damage, loss of brain cells, and gout.

Alcoholics Anonymous (AA) is an effective approach to recovery for those who are willing to work its program. The Twelve Steps and Twelve Traditions of AA provide many with a life structure leading to sobriety. However, AA is criticized by some as being too spiritual. Other treatment alternatives include in-patient care, group counseling, and individual counseling. Behavioral approaches may be helpful for some clients who abuse alcohol. Insight approaches may be beneficial as well.

Nicotine is believed to be the most addictive substance. Found in cigarettes, cigars, snuff, and chewing tobacco, nicotine appears to have antidepressant qualities. Tobacco abuse is very difficult to overcome—counseling, involvement in a support group, and medication (such as Zyban) is frequently needed. Behavioral and insight approaches seem to be the most effective paths to treatment.

Marijuana is a plant that is dried and smoked. Today, marijuana is significantly stronger than it was several decades ago. Marijuana grown in different parts of the world may be more potent than that grown in other parts of the world. People who use marijuana often report intense hunger and drowsiness. Also reported are rapid heart rates, paranoia, and a lack of motivation. Marijuana is occasionally prescribed as a painkiller and appetite enhancer for people with certain terminal illnesses.

Cocaine is snorted, smoked, or injected. When injected, there is a risk of transmission of HIV (see **AIDS/HIV**) and other blood-borne pathogens if a needle is shared. Cocaine is a highly addictive stimulant. Cocaine users report that intensely pleasurable highs are followed by incredibly painful lows. To avoid these lows, cocaine abusers will do almost anything to get their next high. Feelings of invincibility and paranoia are common.

Huffing is the inhalation of fumes from household products and chemicals such as gasoline, paint, nail polish, spray paint propellant, glue, cleaning products, and Freon. Frequently used by children and adolescents as a method of getting high, huffing may cause permanent brain damage and death from either the first use or repeated uses. Huffing is of particular concern because young people use materials easily available in almost any home or store—products that are legal both to buy and to possess. Teaching young people about respecting their bodies and effective decision making helps them learn to avoid the dangers of huffing. For young people who are huffing, in-patient treatment followed up with extensive counseling will be necessary.

The Substance Abuse Subtle Screening Inventory (SASSI) is an exceptional screening tool for substance abuse issues.

Documentation

Reports of substance abuse should be documented in accordance with your agency's policy.

Ethical Considerations

Clients who appear to be intoxicated or impaired during a session may need alternative transportation home. It is also important to set boundaries on sobriety before and during the counseling sessions.

Substance abuse by young people should be reported to Child Protective Services unless the young person is in a substance abuse treatment program.

Further Reading

Thombs, D. L. (1999). *Introduction to addictive behaviors* (2nd ed.). New York: Guilford.

Suicide

Important Considerations

Even with our most compassionate, ethical, and caring efforts, suicide will occur. Assessing suicidality is challenging, stressful, and has no guarantees. Consult with your colleagues. Ask the client about her or his previous attempts. Document your assessment, evaluation, and treatment planning.

Signs and Symptoms

The assessment of lethality has eight facets:

1. Giving away prized possessions/accomplishing final acts
2. Degree of isolation
3. Intensity of depression
4. Previous suicide attempts
5. Having a plan (detail and reversibility)
6. Alcohol and drug abuse
7. Previous psychiatric treatment or hospitalization
8. Availability and use of support system

Intervention

Listen carefully to what the client is saying, with specific attention to her or his affect and determination. Increased depression and isolation, along with the giving away of prized possessions/final acts (e.g., suddenly creating a will, settling accounts, etc.), alcohol and drug abuse (previous or current), and previous psychiatric treatment or hospitalization increases the likelihood of death. If the client is hopeful that the future will be better than her or his present, and is confident that these feelings are only temporary, the potential lethality decreases. Use the Suicide Assessment Checklist (see **Suicide Assessment Checklist**) to assist your evaluation.

Pay particular attention to the client's plan. Use open-ended, direct questions to find out about the client's plan (e.g., "When was the last time you thought about killing yourself?" "How did you plan to kill yourself?" etc.). *The more detailed the client's plan is and the less reversible it is, the more lethal the plan becomes.* For example, situations like this have a high lethality: the client is considering suicide by firearm, recently bought a gun and bullets, has contemplated writing a suicide note, and plans to attempt next week when his children are at school and his significant other is at work.

If you evaluate the situation as highly lethal and your counseling center does not provide emergency services (e.g., temporary hospitalization, medication, etc.), you must refer the client to an appropriate agency. You must also ensure that the client goes to this agency (e.g., arrange transportation with that agency, call the police department or ambulance service, follow the client there in your car, etc.). If the client has the death instrument (e.g., gun, knife, pills, poison, etc.) with her or him, you may need to call the police to separate the suicidal client from the weapon. For your own safety, never attempt to take a weapon from a client.

If the situation is highly lethal and the client refuses treatment, the situation may be serious enough to pursue involuntary commitment. Check with your supervisor for the appropriate procedure at your agency and the laws governing this action in your state.

Documentation

Use the Suicide Assessment Checklist (see **Suicide Assessment Checklist**) to assess the client's potential lethality. Request that the client sign a "No-Suicide" contract (see **Useful Forms and Phone Numbers**). Add these completed forms to the client's file. Record your assessment, evaluation, intervention, and referral in the client's casenotes (see **Casenotes**).

Ethical Considerations

Assess and document potential lethality. Refer for services as appropriate.

Consult with your supervisor immediately; do not wait until your next supervision appointment.

Further Reading

Bongar, B., Berman, A. L., Maris, R. W., Silverman, M. M., Harris, E. A., & Packman, W. L. (Eds.). (1998). *Risk management with suicidal patients*. New York: Guilford Press.
Living Works Education, *Suicide intervention handbook*. (1999). Calgary, AB: Author.

Notes

_____

_____

_____

_____

_____

_____

_____

_____

_____

_____

_____

PART TWO

Alphabetical Index of Counselor Information

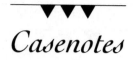

Casenotes

Each client's file is a history of her or his experiences with your counseling agency or practice. Although writing high-quality casenotes is time-consuming, it is also important. Casenotes serve as a record for other counselors who may meet with your client in an emergency or when your client transitions to another counselor. Other counselors can best help the client when your casenotes are legible, efficient, accurate, and detailed. Write your casenotes as soon after the session as possible. In addition to casenotes, the client's file should contain a copy of all handouts you give the client, your completed intake, all forms you ask the client to sign, and other agency paperwork.

What to Include in a Casenote

- Date
- Length of session
- Type of session
- Who attended
- What was discussed
- Interventions
- Location
- Reports of abuse
- Clinical impressions
- Affect
- Evaluation of client's safety
- Handouts and forms
- Plan for continued progress
- Next appointment
- Phone calls
- Test results
- Suggested reading
- Referrals
- Reports you make to other agencies (e.g., child abuse)
- Your signature (full name and credentials; must be legible)

If your counseling agency or practice keeps electronic client files, you should document everything in the list above and retain master copies of handouts in the event that an actual copy of the latter is needed.

Your casenotes should be useful not only to you but also to your supervisor and to anyone who may work with this client in the future. Before writing casenotes, ask yourself what information you would like to know about the session if you had never worked with this client before. Your casenotes should also be useful to you in court. A state or federal court of law can subpoena client files if legal action is taken against you or your client. Write your casenotes so you or another counselor can use them in the future. Never remove any material from a client's file at any time for any reason.

Remember, a client may ask to review her or his file at any time.

Further Reading

Mitchell, R. (2001). *Documentation in counseling records* (2nd ed.). Washington, DC: American Counseling Association.

Consultation

Consultation is a different experience from supervision. Your supervisor has a legal responsibility for your clients. The consultant does not have a legal responsibility for your clients. Your supervisor is, most likely, an excellent source of information and guidance for the further development of your counseling skills. Most supervisors work with many counselors and interns and possess specialized knowledge in a particular area of counseling. You may need a consultant when you encounter a client with needs that you and your supervisor are not prepared to meet. A consultant is an expert in a particular area (e.g., substance abuse, family violence, or depression).

Consultation can be formal or informal. In formal consultation, you arrange to meet on a regular basis with the consultant. Although you may discuss the client with the consultant, the consultant's obligation is to you, to help you build your skills and knowledge base so that you can effectively help your clients. Consultation may also be informal. In informal consultation you might visit with a colleague from time to time, and during these brief meetings, the consultant would teach you about her or his area of expertise.

Consultants are all around you: your colleagues, your doctor, your pastor or rabbi, or your child's teacher. You can learn from these many sources without divulging any confidential client information. If you use a consultant outside of your agency, you should check with your supervisor regarding what information about the client you can share with the consultant.

Before meetings with a consultant, spend a few moments to consider what information you need from the consultant to effectively help your client. Remember that the consultant's obligation is to help you develop *your* skills, so consider what skills need developing. You may also want to ask your supervisor or another trusted colleague who would be a good consultant to help you meet your needs.

As a new counselor, you will likely have the need for frequent consultation. As time progresses, it is likely that you will become a consultant to other counselors.

Further Reading

Dougherty, M. A. (1995). *Consultation: Practice and perspectives in school and community settings* (2nd ed.). Pacific Grove, CA: Brooks/Cole.

Couple and Family Systems

Today's families take a wide variety of forms, and the competent counselor needs to be prepared to meet with any form she or he is presented. All counselors need a basic understanding of couple and family systems, even if the counselor only works with individuals. All of our clients grew up in some kind of family, and their experiences in that family have impacted their present experiences. Most clients live in a family they created or, at least, with another person. Some clients live alone.

Counselors will meet with couples and families experiencing communication problems, couples and families who are divorcing, couples considering marriage or commitment, couples struggling with infidelity, gay and lesbian couples and families, interracial couples and families, single parents with children, and more. The list of concerns the couple or family seeking counseling may have is limited only by your imagination.

The fundamental difference between counseling couples and families and counseling individuals is that the counselor working with couples and families works with the system and the relationships in that system rather than just with the individuals. The *interaction* between members of the couple or family is counseled, as opposed to one person's perceptions of the couple or family interactions. Couple and family counseling presents the counselor with unique opportunities for helping the couple or family system.

In general, systems approaches conceptualize psychopathology as an expression of problems within the relationship rather than representing the mental challenges of an individual (see **Systems Approaches**). The person with the "mental disorder" is called the identified patient, or "IP" for short. The IP is viewed as the person whom the family or couple has elected to go and seek help. The counselor who ordinarily works with individuals often works with IPs. The systems counselor wants to meet with the entire family or with both members of the couple. The systems counselor's goal is to relieve symptoms in the individual through the system.

To remain effective, the counselor must avoid being triangulated into the couple or any of the family relationships. The counselor must be respectful and neutral if she or he is to help the family. The counselor must be close enough to help the couple or family and, at the same time, to maintain appropriate boundaries. Through interaction with the effective counselor, the couple or family system changes through experiencing new ways of interacting with each other.

As with any other approach to counseling, it is important to ask yourself, "When is couple and family-system counseling appropriate?" Using a systems approach is often very helpful to the couple or family; however, this approach may not always be appropriate with every family. For example, couples and families experiencing domestic violence or sexual abuse (see **Domestic Violence, Sexual Abuse**) should receive separate counseling—especially during the initial treatment phases—for safety reasons. If the client who is being abused discloses this information in a joint session with the counselor, that person leaves the session in great danger of being further abused. The interactional aspects of the system can be dealt with best after the abuser receives group and individual counseling. The person being abused is often better able to handle the interactional aspects of the relationship after group and individual counseling as well.

Further Reading

Becvar, D. S., & Becvar, R. J. (1999). *Family therapy: A systemic integration.* Boston: Allyn & Bacon.

Donnovan, J. M. (Ed.). (1999). *Short-term couple therapy.* New York: Guilford.

Huntley, D. K. (1995). *Understanding stepfamilies: Implications for assessment and treatment.* Washington, DC: American Counseling Association.

Stevens-Smith, P., & Hughes, M. M. (1993). *Legal issues in marriage and family counseling.* Washington, DC: American Counseling Association.

▼▼▼
Developing Your Own Approach

Becoming a counselor is a journey—an ongoing process. You started your advanced internship with a set of skills and ideas developed in graduate school. Now you are combining these classroom experiences with counseling experiences. It is likely you are exploring what is comfortable to you, as well as discovering some methods that do not seem as useful in your area of practice.

You are meeting with your clients, going to supervision, and consulting with your colleagues. Clients are presenting you with concerns that sounded a lot easier to deal with when you were in class. You are becoming a problem solver, a guide, and maybe even a coach. Counseling requires knowledge, skills, and the ability to think both quickly and creatively. To help a client meet her or his needs, you combine your conceptualization of that person with your knowledge, skills, and experiences. All of your experiences can be a part of your approach to counseling if you are willing to consider how the pieces of who you are fit together and how these pieces can help another person.

The most effective counseling approaches combine education and experience, stay flexible to the situation, and continue to grow and develop. For your professional vitality and the well-being of your clients, you should continue to refine and polish your approach to counseling across the length of your career.

Here are a few questions to consider as you continue to develop your own approach:

1. What motivates clients to seek counseling? To change their lives?
2. What do I believe about the nature (e.g., inherent goodness, ability to change) of clients?
3. What components of the different theoretical approaches do I like to use? Why?
4. What components of the different theoretical approaches do I avoid? Why?
5. How directive am I as a counselor?
6. What do I believe about the power of the counseling relationship?
7. What role does educating the client play in counseling?
8. What role does religion and spirituality play in counseling?
9. How do I feel about unmarried people who live together?
10. How do I feel about working with people who are gay, lesbian, bisexual, or transgendered?
11. How much do I know about cultures other than my own?
12. What motivates some clients to abuse alcohol, drugs, sex, or gaming?
13. How self-sufficient do I want my clients to be?
14. What role does stewardship play in counseling?
15. What training experiences do I need to become a more effective counselor?

Further Reading

Hazler, R. J., & Kottler, J. A. (1994). *The emerging professional counselor: Student dreams to professional realities.* Washington, DC: American Counseling Association.

DSM-IV-TR Use

The *Diagnostic and Statistical Manual of Mental Disorders* (2000) is a valuable tool in your work as a counselor. Appropriate use of the *DSM-IV-TR* requires training, experience, and practice. Before using the *DSM-IV-TR*, read the introductory material found on pages xxiii–37 of the *DSM-IV-TR*. Consult your supervisor and/or colleagues when you have questions about making a diagnosis.

A *DSM-IV-TR* diagnosis has potent effects for clients. For some clients it brings relief—for perhaps the first time, they know what they are experiencing is called and, as a result, can seek treatment for it. For many clients, a *DSM-IV-TR* diagnosis means third-party reimbursement. A diagnosis can have other important effects, such as preventing a client from gaining future employment or from receiving disability payments from Social Security.

A diagnosis should be parsimonious, should accurately reflect the client's experiences and situation, and should be reviewed frequently and updated as necessary. As you know, a client's file is a history of her or his experiences in counseling. Many practitioners will review the diagnosis to get a thumbnail sketch of the client. However, this practice is not advisable. Although knowing a client's diagnosis is helpful, it is important to realize that there are as many unique forms of depression (or any other diagnosable condition) as there are people with depression. Every client is unique, and so are her or his counseling needs. There is no one "cure all" for any diagnosable condition. How you will help a client depends not only on the diagnosis but also on the client's experiences, personality, needs, and goals. Counselors treat the whole person.

The Decision Trees for Differential Diagnosis found in the *DSM-IV-TR* (beginning on page 745) are highly useful for defining a diagnosis more clearly. Whether or not you use the Decision Trees to make a diagnosis, you must consider the client's cultural heritage as it impacts the diagnosis. Important cultural factors can include ethnicity, age, and sexual orientation.

The *DSM-IV-TR* is divided into 27 sections:

- Disorders usually first diagnosed in infancy, childhood, or adolescence
- Delirium, dementia, and amnestic and other cognitive disorders
- Mental disorders due to a general medical condition
- Substance-related disorders
- Schizophrenia and other psychotic disorders
- Mood disorders
- Somatoform disorders
- Factitious disorders
- Disassociative disorders
- *DSM-IV* classification (with ICD-10 codes)
- Outline for cultural formulation and glossary of culture-bound syndromes
- Anxiety disorders
- Sexual and gender identity disorders
- Eating disorders
- Sleep disorders
- Impulse-control disorders not elsewhere classified
- Adjustment disorders
- Personality disorders
- Other conditions that may be a focus of clinical attention
- Additional codes

- Decision trees
- Criteria sets and axes provided for further study
- Glossary
- Highlights of changes in the *DSM-IV-TR*
- Alphabetical listing of *DSM-IV-TR* diagnostic codes
- Numerical listing of *DSM-IV-TR* diagnostic codes
- ICD-9-CM codes for selected general medical conditions and medication-induced disorders

A *DSM-IV-TR* diagnosis is made on five axes. Each axis serves a different purpose and, as appropriate, you should make a diagnosis for your clients on each axis. Briefly, the axes are

Axis I:	Clinical disorders and other conditions that may be the focus of clinical attention
Axis II:	Personality disorders and mental retardation
Axis III:	General medical conditions
Axis IV:	Psychosocial and environmental problems
Axis V:	Global assessment of functioning

For thorough definition of the axes, see the *DSM-IV-TR*, pages 27–34.

Further Reading

Morrison, J. (1995). *The DSM-IV made easy: The clinician's guide to diagnosis.* New York: Guilford.

▼▼▼
Ethics

Every profession, especially complicated ones like health care, law, and counseling, needs a guiding light. Each of these professions shares at least one element in common: gray spaces. Gray spaces are those areas where decision making is challenging. A code of ethics helps the practitioner function when it becomes difficult to make decisions. There are many counseling situations you may encounter where ethical decision making will be involved. For example, a client is impressed with your work together and brings you a gift. Do you accept it? A client is no longer paying for her or his sessions. What can you do? How can you advertise your services? A client threatens to kill himself and says he is merely "joking." What should you do?

Situations such as these are difficult to resolve because what may seem like a good idea—for example, helping a client in a desperate financial situation through buying catalog products she sells—may, in fact, be an ethical violation that could place you in professional or legal jeopardy. Failure to follow established ethical guidelines could result in the loss of your professional license or bring about expensive, time-consuming, and possibly embarrassing trials. When you are presented with situations that involve ethical choices, consider your options carefully and proceed with caution.

As you encounter situations in which you are unsure of how to proceed, the best action you can take is to meet with your supervisor or another trusted colleague and discuss your concerns. When you talk with others about your ethical concerns, share with them how you think the counseling relationship may be affected, what you are afraid may happen, and what solutions you think may work. Frequently, your colleagues who have some professional distance from your situation can be more objective and help you plan an appropriate, ethical course of action. *No book replaces consultations with your supervisors and colleagues when you have ethical concerns.*

Although codes of ethics vary between professional organizations, there are several general ethical guidelines you can follow:

- Understand and apply the limits of confidentiality as they relate to individual, group, and family counseling.
- Avoid dual relationships (e.g., meeting a client for coffee, buying products from a client, or entering into business relationships with a client).
- Use only those psychological assessments that you are qualified to use.
- Never have any sexual contact with a client or former client.
- Identify and seek help when you have personal counseling needs.
- Refer clients when you are not qualified to meet their needs.
- Do not accept gifts from clients or engage in bartering for services with clients.

You are encouraged to read the full code of ethics for your professional association and counseling agency or practice. The American Counseling Association has a comprehensive code. You can obtain a copy of the *ACA Code of Ethics and Standards of Practice* by calling the ACA at 800-422-2648.

Your state licensing board and place of employment may have additional requirements.

Further Reading

Herlihy, B., & Corey, G. (1996). *ACA ethical standards casebook* (5th ed.). Washington, DC: American Counseling Association.

Genograms

Genograms communicate a wealth of information about the client very efficiently. Systems theorists (see **Systems Approaches**) use genograms to track alliances, conflicts, and other family history such as divorces, deaths, and ages. (See Figure 2.1.)

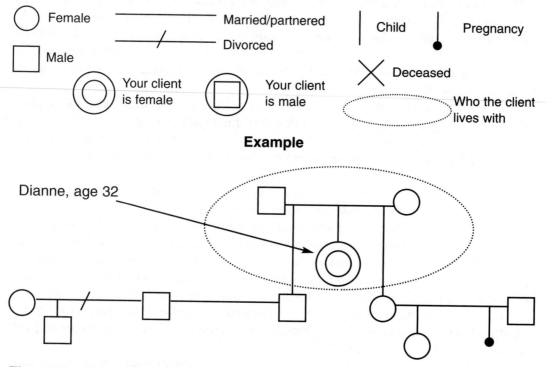

Figure 2.1. Frequently used genogram symbols with an example

Explanation

The example indicates three generations. The client, Dianne, is a 32-year-old female, middle-born child, and she lives with her parents. She has an older brother and a younger sister. Her older brother is gay and is in a partnered relationship with a man who was previously married and has a son. Her younger sister is pregnant, married, and has a daughter. Both of the client's parents are living.

Questions You Might Have While Creating the Genogram

1. Why does the client live with her parents?
2. How does she describe her relationships with her parents?
3. How does she describe her relationships with her brother, his son, his partner, and his ex-wife?
4. How does she describe her relationships with her sister, her sister's husband, and her sister's daughter?

Use

Genograms are helpful in supervision as you communicate with your team about the client. Genograms are also helpful in refreshing your memory about the client. Finally, genograms are also valuable for other counselors who meet with the client, because the genogram provides a snapshot of the family.

Further Reading

McGoldrick, M., Gerson, R., & Shellenberger, S. (1999). *Genograms: Assessment and intervention.* New York: Norton.

Human Growth and Development

Human growth and development is an important topic for both counselors and clients. Counselors often use the perspective provided by human growth and development to understand their clients better. Clients can use this perspective to enhance their understanding of their own lives and the lives of their children. For many people, learning about what children are able to do as a normal part of human development provides them with insight.

In Part 3, you will find information about each of the major theories of counseling. *These counseling theories are also theories of human development.* So instead of looking at the pragmatics of growth and development, let us take a look at how you might use what I call the "Human Development Perspective" in your practice.

When you are working with clients, how often do you stop to consider the client's stage of development (including physical, mental, and emotional development)? Some presenting "problems" are the result of either slowed or advanced development and could be addressed through the Human Development Perspective. Through this perspective, you might take a psychoeducational approach to help your client better understand herself or himself. This approach may help relieve anxiety and tension for your client and your client's family. Often, it can be helpful to know that the ability to do certain things will develop with time or that the loss of certain abilities is normal with age and that everyone is on her or his own timetable.

The Human Development Perspective does not suggest that a psychoeducational approach is all that is needed. Rather, it suggests looking at the challenges our clients face through a different lens. For example, if a client is concerned about recent memory losses and your clinical interview leads you to believe that this is a result of the normal aging process, you might approach this client and the client's family through offering them help coping with the loss, education about the aging process, and strategies to improve living. This could be a vastly different approach from teaching a client's family member to express her or his frustration about the memory loss to the person with the memory loss.

Another example might be in work with parents frustrated with their children. Some parents have unrealistic expectations about children's abilities and benefit greatly from learning about development and developing communication skills to help them communicate with their children's actual developmental stage—rather than the developmental level the parent wishes the children were at.

You might also use the Human Development Perspective to help you visualize a client's growth through the counseling process. For example, I have found this perspective helpful in understanding women who have been battered as they move from victim to survivor to thriver.

Further Reading

Santrock, J. W. (1995). *Life-span development* (5th ed.). Madison, WI: WCB, Brown & Benchmark.

Psychological Assessment

Psychological assessment is a valuable tool for clients and counselors. Assessment instruments can put into words concerns a client may not be able to verbalize. Assessments, in addition to clinical interviews, can help develop a diagnosis and treatment plan. Assessment instruments exist for just about anything, including intelligence, career planning, depression, anxiety, suicidality, personality, substance abuse, and domestic violence. Assessments come in many forms, including self-reports, projective testing, and formal interviews.

Because psychological assessment can be very costly and time-consuming, care needs to be used when recommending and administering assessments. Assessment instruments should be carefully selected for their appropriateness for each particular client, based upon the client's needs, wants, experiences, cultural identity, and other personal characteristics.

Professional counselors may use only those assessment instruments that they are qualified to use by virtue of their professional education. Administering a test when you are not qualified to do so places you in ethical and legal jeopardy. Each psychological assessment instrument is graded for the educational qualifications necessary to administer that test, as seen in Figure 2.2, which displays the usual requirements for each level of test. Test publishers and state licensing boards may have additional requirements.

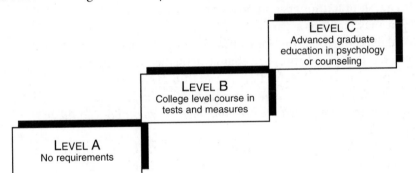

Figure 2.2. Requirements for assessment-instrument administration

Before administering any assessment instrument, you should review and understand the instructions and scoring manual that come with the test. Assessment instruments, and the manuals and scoring templates that come with them, may not be photocopied because the authors of the instrument receive compensation only for those instruments that are ordered from the test publisher. Not only is photocopying assessment instruments unethical, it is also a violation of copyright laws.

The results of psychological assessments must be explained to each client in language she or he can understand. The results of assessments are confidential and should be added to the client's file.

If you feel an assessment that you are not qualified to administer would be beneficial, you must refer the client to a qualified practitioner for evaluation (see **Useful Forms and Phone Numbers**).

Further Reading

Hood, A. B., & Johnson, R. W. (1997). *Assessment in counseling: A guide to the use of psychological assessment procedures.* Washington, DC: American Counseling Association.

Psychopharmacology

Most people take medications either on an occasional or a recurring basis. Today, doctors prescribe a wide variety of medications. Some of these prescribed medications are for psychological concerns, such as depression (see **Depression**) or anxiety (see **Anxiety**). Other prescribed medications may have psychological side effects when taken or when the course of medication ends. Over-the-counter medications may also have psychological side effects.

You should ask your clients about the medications they take, how much they take, when they take them, and why. Often it is helpful to ask the client to bring the bottles for all medications she or he takes to your office. Then you can record the correct spelling of the medication, dosage, instructions, and prescriber information in the client's file. Dramatic changes in client affect, thinking, and/or behavior may be related to changes in medication. Having this information in the client's file provides you with additional historical information to assist you in the counseling process. Consult the *Physician's Desk Reference* for detailed information about the action, effects, and side effects of prescribed medications.

Only physicians and psychiatrists may prescribe medications. However, under a doctor's supervision, nurse-practitioners and physician's assistants may also prescribe medications. Although you may feel that a particular medication may benefit a client, the doctor will make the final decision about the appropriateness of the medication, if any, and the needed dosage. If you feel that medication or a change in medication is appropriate, refer your client to a qualified physician (see **Useful Forms and Phone Numbers**). *Never instruct a client to stop taking medication or to change the dosage of a medication. If a client appears to be responding poorly to a prescribed medication, refer the client back to the prescriber for additional evaluation.*

There are three classes of prescribed medications that counselors frequently encounter: antidepressants, antipsychotics, and tranquilizers (See Table 2.1).

Further Reading

Bezchilibnyk-Butler, K. Z., & Jeffries, J. J. (Eds.). (2000). *Clinical handbook of psychotropic drugs* (10th ed.). Seattle, WA: Hogrefe & Huber Publishers.

Konopasek, D. E. (2000). *Medication fact sheets: A medication reference guide for the non-medical professional.* Anchorage, AK: Arctic Tern Publishing.

Table 2.1 Types of Prescribed Medications

Antidepressants[1]	Antipsychotics[2]	Tranquilizers[3]
Selective serotonin-reuptake inhibitors (SSRI) are frequently prescribed to elevate mood and alleviate symptoms (e.g., lethargy, suicidal ideation, etc.); monoamine oxidase inhibitors (MAOI), tricyclics, and heterocyclics are also prescribed.	Antipsychotic medications are frequently prescribed to relieve and/or manage the symptoms (e.g., disorganized thinking, psychotic thinking, etc.) of schizophrenia, bipolar disorder, and cyclothymia.	Benzodiazepines, or tranquilizers, are frequently prescribed to relieve symptoms of anxiety (e.g., nervousness, worry, etc.).

Commonly prescribed medications		Commonly prescribed medications		Commonly prescribed medications	
Brand name	**Generic name**	**Brand name**	**Generic name**	**Brand name**	**Generic name**
Paxil	paroxetine	Clozaril	clozapine	Ativan	lorazepam
Prozac	fluoxetine	Haldol	haloperidol	BuSpar	buspirone
Serzone	nefazodone	Navane	thiothixene	Valium	diazepam
Wellbutrin	bupropion	Risperidal	risperidone	Xanax	alprazolam

[1]Antidepressants are also used in the treatment of alcoholism, anorexia, anxiety, bulimia, dysthymia, insomnia, obsessive-compulsive disorder, panic disorder, post-traumatic stress disorder, and schizophrenia.

[2]Clients taking antipsychotic medications should visit their doctor frequently for physical examination. Most antipsychotic medications have numerous side effects (e.g., dizziness, flat affect, nausea).

[3]Benzodiazepines are also used in the treatment of bipolar disorder, panic attacks, depression, and phobias. Benzodiazepines can become addictive when taken for a long period of time or when taken incorrectly.

Social and Cultural Considerations

Never forget the importance of culture. Many counseling approaches have been criticized for defining Anglo male behavior as acceptable and appropriate. In our work with clients, we must remember that our clients' cultural heritage impacts their styles of thinking, feeling, behavior, and interacting with others.

Culture is not limited only to ethnicity. Age groups (such as teens), sexual identity groups (such as gay males), and religious groups (such as Roman Catholics) may have their own cultural identity as well. The best way to discover how a client's culture impacts her or him is to listen carefully and ask the client. The ethical counselor must also consider how her or his culture impacts the counseling process. It is critically important to avoid stereotypes. Although different profiles have been offered for different cultural groups, many clients will not fit the mold. This makes sense if you consider your own development; you may strongly identify with various aspects of several cultures. This is true of many of our clients as well.

Here are a few questions you may wish to consider:

1. What messages did I learn as a child about other cultures?
2. What do I say under my breath about others while driving?
3. What jokes do I find amusing? Why?
4. How much do I believe my culture is "right" and other cultures are "wrong"?
5. What do I associate with the word *culture*?
6. How does my colloquial speech suggest how I feel about other cultures?
7. What is the appropriate method of emotional expression?
8. How much personal space does a person need?
9. How do other cultures demonstrate respect?

Further Reading

Okun, B. F., Fried, J., & Okun, M. L. (1999). *Understanding diversity: A learning-as-practice primer.* Pacific Grove, CA: Brooks/Cole.

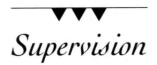

Supervision

Supervision takes a variety of forms, usually group supervision (more common) and individual supervision (less common). Not to be overlooked are the frequent informal supervisions that occur on a more regular basis. How you use supervision is up to you. It depends on your needs, your client's needs, and your supervisor's abilities. Staffing your cases and training are the primary purposes of supervision. You should plan on staffing each of your clients at least once a month, and more frequently if you are experiencing difficulty with a client, if a client is in crisis, or if your work setting requires more. Frequently, counselors talk about areas where they feel stuck with their clients—presenting ethical concerns, issues with client dynamics, and problems where they feel they have little experience. Supervision is also a place to share client success stories and for you to grow personally as well as professionally.

When you staff a case, take the client's file with you. Share with the group basic information about your client: name, age, occupation, presenting problem, current plan for progress, and what help you need. You may record in the client's casenotes that you staffed the case, as well as any specific suggestions you received from your colleagues. Have your supervisor sign the client's file to document when it was staffed.

Not to be discounted are the more frequent, informal supervisions and consultations that occur casually between counselors. Typically these encounters last only a few minutes and focus on a specific need (e.g., information about substance abuse or suicide). These brief meetings are an important source of information for the busy counselor; however, they do not replace attending formal supervision.

Whether you deal with individual, group, or informal supervision, make sure you and your colleagues take steps to protect the privacy of your clients. Talking about a client in a hallway is not appropriate because of the possibility that another client will overhear your conversation. In addition to jeopardizing a client's confidentiality, you also set a poor example for other counselors and trainees. Practices such as this (even if you leave out names and other identifying information), when heard by clients, frequently leave them wondering where it is you are talking about *them*. Before talking about a client, ask yourself, "Who is listening to this conversation?"

Consult your state licensing board regarding the requirements for becoming a clinical supervisor.

Further Reading

Disney, M. J., & Stephens, A. M. (1994). *Legal issues in clinical supervision.* Washington, DC: American Counseling Association.

Kaiser, T. L. (1997). *Supervisory relationships: Exploring the human element.* Pacific Grove, CA: Brooks/Cole.

▼▼▼
Testifying in Court

Testifying in court is a frightening prospect for some counselors. Other counselors enjoy going to court and assisting their clients. However you feel, one thing is sure: it is likely that you will be asked to appear in court at some time during your professional counseling career. I require a subpoena before I will appear in court; you should check with your employer regarding the conditions under which you may testify in court. Before you are ever asked to appear in court, you may wish to accompany a colleague to court when she or he testifies to familiarize yourself with what happens, hear how questions are asked, and acclimate yourself to the atmosphere of a courtroom. If this is not possible, you might consider watching a trial on Court TV.

When appearing in court, you should always dress appropriately for that court. If you are not sure what is acceptable in that court and what is not, call ahead and find out. Counselors appearing in court should, at a minimum, wear a shirt and tie or blouse, and dress pants or a skirt. Always address the judge as "Your Honor," not as "Judge."

Answer the question asked of you, not the question you wished had been asked. Do not volunteer additional information. Speak clearly and look at the jury as you answer; sit still and keep your hands in your lap. If an attorney objects—stop. Do not say another word until the judge makes a decision regarding the objection. If you do not understand a question, ask the judge for clarification. All questions must be answered audibly. Take a complete copy of the client's file with you and review the file before going to court. If you feel you need to refer to the file before answering, ask the judge if you may do so. Answer all questions honestly, even if your answer is not flattering to your client.

It is okay to think about your possible testimony ahead of time; however, it is important that you speak naturally while on the stand. Avoid sounding as though you are reading from a script. To help you remain calm, you might consider asking a trusted colleague to accompany you. No matter how a question is asked of you, remain professional, pleasant, and calm. Remember that it is the opposing attorney's *job* to attempt to discredit you or "bend" your testimony—it is not personal.

Further Reading

Remley, Jr., T. P. (1991). *Preparing for court appearances.* Washington, DC: American Counseling Association.
Weikel, W. J., & Hughes, P. R. (1993). *The counselor as expert witness.* Washington, DC: American Counseling Association.

Notes

_____

_____

_____

_____

_____

_____

PART THREE

Alphabetical Index of Selected Theories

Overview

Counseling theories help us organize our thinking about the challenges our clients face, and about how we can help them grow and change. Whatever theories you prefer to use with your clients, it is critical that as a counselor you keep your eyes open to other possibilities. Any theory acts both as a guide and as a pair of blinders. How open are you to other possible explanations of your clients' behavior? Is your theoretical perspective helping or hindering your clients?

Supervision and consultation are excellent environments for obtaining other perspectives on understanding your clients. There is no one "right" theory or approach for working with any particular client. Over time, many counselors blend several theories together and develop their own unique approach for working with clients. When creating your unique blend, you should consider your own development and needs. Are your personal struggles preventing you from helping clients with particular concerns?

Although different approaches are covered very briefly in this text, I suggest you review either or both of these resources:

Corey, G. (1996). *Theory and practice of counseling and psychotherapy* (5th ed.). Pacific Grove, CA: Brooks/Cole.
Prochaska, J. O., & Norcross, J. C. (1994). *Systems of psychotherapy: A transtheoretical analysis* (3rd ed.). Pacific Grove, CA: Brooks/Cole.

New approaches for working with clients continue to be developed. I encourage you to study and consult with other professionals before trying a new approach. Some questions you may want to ask are

1. Is this approach ethical?
2. How will this approach help my client?
3. Will this approach encourage my client to avoid problems?
4. What research supports this approach?
5. Is there another approach that will help my client reach her or his goals?
6. What do I know about how to use this approach?
7. What risks are associated with this approach?
8. What light will this approach shine on my client's world?
9. What are this approach's blind spots?

For a review of the counseling process, refer to

Teyber, E. (1992). *Interpersonal process in psychotherapy: A guide for clinical training* (2nd ed.). Pacific Grove, CA: Brooks/Cole.

For a review of counseling techniques, see

Okun, B. F. (2002). *Effective helping: Interviewing and counseling techniques* (6th ed.). Pacific Grove, CA: Brooks/Cole.

Adlerian Approach

A contemporary of Freud, Alfred Adler developed an approach to counseling that differs in several significant ways from the psychoanalytic approach (see **Psychoanalytic Approach**). Chief among these differences is Adler's focus on the conscious, phenomenology, and the striving for superiority. Like Freud, Adler's theory of counseling and human development, often called Individual Psychology, continues to influence the development of new theories. Adler's theory can be used with individuals, groups, couples, and families.

Foundation

Adlerian theory is founded on the concepts of *life goal* and *social interest* (Corey, 1996). A person's life goal motivates her or his behavior. These goals are not usually of the "I need to buy a house" variety. Rather, life goals address core personality issues and concerns, such as "When I am in control of those around me I am safe." Social interest refers to a person's knowledge of her or his impact on the world in which she or he lives. A person with a healthy social interest has less intense feelings of inferiority and is more likely to appropriately meet her or his life goal.

Striving for superiority is often misunderstood. Adler does not suggest that people should try to be superior over others; rather, he suggests that individuals strive to overcome their own self-perceived weaknesses. An individual's birth order (see **Birth Order/Parenting**) points to the roots of some of these self-perceived weaknesses, and as a result, to the individual's life goal.

Techniques

The Adlerian approach seeks to address ineffective life goals and replace them with effective ones. The fundamental tool used by Adlerian counselors is the counseling relationship. Other tools include working with lifestyle analysis, early memories, dreams, and the family constellation. The lifestyle analysis is used to explore the client's perceptions about her or his life experiences. Early memories are explored and reviewed to help the client and the counselor better understand the client's lifestyle. Dreams are evaluated for their significance for current treatment and future choices. A family constellation is much more than a genogram (see **Genograms**). The constellation explores the quality of family-of-origin relationships, how these relationships influenced the client's development, birth order, perceptions of family roles, and how these relationships and childhood experiences affect current functioning.

Adlerian counselors always focus on the relationship and on encouraging the client. The tools above are often used, but not as a replacement for a meaningful, professional human relationship between counselor and client. Adlerian counselors believe in the power of the counseling relationship to encourage growth and change. A primary way this occurs is through the use of immediacy—addressing the relationship dynamics between client and counselor as they occur in the counseling session.

Further Reading

Adler, A. (1989). *Individual psychology: A systematic presentation in selections from his writings* (H. L. Ansbacher & R. R. Ansbacher, Eds.). New York: HarperCollins.

Behavioral Approach

Frequently used to treat anxieties, phobias, eating disorders, and sexual issues, the behavioral approach uses the scientific method to offer clients relief from problematic behaviors.

Foundation

Behavioral counselors believe all behavior (adaptive and maladaptive) is learned. Psychopathology is the result of faulty learning. Counseling is used to teach or help the client discover behaviors to correct the faulty learning. Insight is *not* necessary.

Reinforcement, both positive and negative, increases the likelihood that a behavior will be repeated. Punishment, both positive and negative, decreases the likelihood that a behavior will be repeated. Reinforcing desirable behaviors instead of punishing undesirable behaviors is more successful.

Let us take a closer look at reinforcement. Positive reinforcement is the addition of a desirable consequence after a behavior is performed. Negative reinforcement is the removal of an undesirable consequence after a behavior is performed. For example, a parent who wants her child to place dirty clothes in the hamper may reward the child with a point (token economy) each time the child places clothes in the hamper (positive reinforcement). The parent may also reward the child through not nagging about placing the clothes in the hamper (negative reinforcement).

Techniques

Implosive therapy, flooding therapy, thought stopping, and systematic desensitization are used to assist the client in the process of change. Imagined situations are used in implosive therapy. The actual feared stimulus is used in flooding therapy. Thought stopping is used to cease negative self-talk. Systematic desensitization, based on reciprocal inhibition, is used to teach the client to be relaxed in the presence of anxiety-provoking stimuli. Social modeling is used to display appropriate behaviors. With repeated exposure to modeling, it is believed that clients will begin to use the new behaviors.

Token economies are used in the treatment of severe psychological disorders, often in in-patient hospital settings, classroom management, and shaping the behavior of children at home. In a token economy, a contract is established between counselor and client, between parent and child, or between teacher and student. In the contract, the participants agree which behaviors are acceptable, how many points will be rewarded for that behavior, and how the points may be redeemed. To be effective, the token economy is based on positive reinforcement, and the points are redeemed for items of value to the participants. For example, a participant may redeem her or his points for a one-half-hour visit to the library, two video game tokens, an apple, and so on.

Further Reading

Thorpe, G. L., & Olson, S. L. (1997). *Behavior therapy: Concepts, procedures, and applications.* Boston: Allyn & Bacon.

Brief/Solution-Focused Approach

The brief/solution-focused approach (for brevity I call it the brief approach) has, perhaps unjustly, received the harshest criticism of any approach to counseling. This approach is neither devoid of feeling nor uninterested in the client's history. Rather, the brief approach has a different focus, a *focus on solutions* as opposed to a *focus on problems.*

Foundation

If insight by itself were enough to solve a client's problem, she or he would not seek counseling. Many clients have experienced their "problem" for several years before seeking help, and they understand their "problem" thoroughly. The brief approach shifts the focus away from details about the "problem" to information about attempted solutions, helping clients to increase the number of available options they consider, and assisting clients in evaluating their feelings about various alternatives to the "problem."

The counselor focuses on actions the client can take. For example, the counselor might say, "What are you doing about your depression?" rather than "How long have you felt depressed?" The brief approach assumes all clients can solve their problems. The counselor's role lies in helping clients uncover potential solutions. The only solutions that will work for the client are the solutions she or he generates. The counselor does not need to know the details of the "problem" to assist the client in this process. Because the client already understands the details of the "problem," she or he is the single best person to generate solutions.

Techniques

All clients need acknowledgment that they are, in fact, struggling. A counselor using the brief approach needs to listen to the client and convey an understanding of the struggle to the client. To do this, the counselor must also have relationship skills. How the client feels about a potential solution is as important as how a client feels about the "problem."

A wide variety of techniques are used in the brief approach. The goal of all the techniques is to develop potential solutions. Of these techniques, the most famous is probably the Miracle Question. With a Miracle Question, the counselor describes in some detail a scenario in which, usually at night while the client is sleeping, something magical happens and the "problem" is resolved. When you wake up what will be the first signs that the miracle has happened? Scaling is frequently used (often from 0 to 10). The client can scale anything: how severe the "problem" is, how much commitment she or he has to developing solutions, how confident the client is that a solution will be effective, and so on. Exception questions are also used. For example, what is it like when the "problem" is not happening? Other common questions include:

- After the change has happened, how will your [friend, spouse, partner, child, etc.] describe you as different?
- How have you tried to solve this problem?

Goals are always about the client and are always positive. For example, "I'll make my kids stop arguing" is an ineffective goal. An effective goal might be, "I'll choose to teach my children problem-solving skills." Additionally, the brief approach assumes personal agency through questions such as, "How did you get yourself to do that?" or "How did you make that happen?"

Further Reading

Walter, J. L., & Peller, J. E. (1992). *Becoming solution-focused in brief therapy.* New York: Brunner/Mazel.

Existential Approach

The existential approach to counseling is perhaps one of the most powerful approaches to working with clients. Many practitioners developed this approach. Although there is no specific founder of the existential approach, Rollo May and Viktor Frankl are often thought of when the existential approach is mentioned.

Foundation

The focus of the existential approach is on the professional relationship between counselor and client. A counselor who uses the existential approach focuses on the in-the-moment interactions between counselor and client in order to assist the client in making positive change. Some of the anxiety each person experiences is to be expected. However, when anxiety becomes more intense and more pervasive, it is called neurotic anxiety. Neurotic anxiety is not healthy and needs to be addressed in counseling.

In the existential approach, it is assumed that clients have the freedom to create the life she or he wishes. With this freedom comes existential anxiety. Existential anxiety occurs as the client comes to accept the responsibility that accompanies this freedom. To make changes, the client often needs assistance coping with existential anxiety. Existential anxiety is normal and is to be expected.

To facilitate the client's coping with existential anxiety, the counselor assists the client in expanding her or his self-awareness. Increased self-awareness helps the client identify sources of existential anxiety, choices she or he might like to make, the client's uniqueness in the universe, the reality of death, and the all-important concepts of freedom and responsibility. Through increased self-awareness, the client not only becomes better able to manage her or his existential anxiety, she or he also develops a sense of meaning and purposefulness.

Techniques

Although it is likely that existential counselors use a variety of techniques from other theories and approaches, the existential approach has no specific counseling techniques. The key to existential counseling is the relationship, the relationship, and...the relationship.

Further Reading

Cohn, H. W., & Cohn, H. W. (1997). *Existential thought and therapeutic practice: An introduction to existential psychotherapy.* Thousand Oaks, CA: Sage.

Gestalt Approach

The Gestalt approach, formulated primarily by Fritz Perls, is related to the existential approach. A powerful approach to working with clients, the Gestalt approach is best experienced as a client before being used as a counselor.

Foundation

The most important tool of the Gestalt approach is the counselor as a person expressed through the current experiencing in the counselor/client relationship. Although techniques are used in the Gestalt approach, they are less important than the counseling relationship itself.

Clients are encouraged to experience their emotions fully rather than to talk about them. Clients may be hesitant to experience their emotions, fearing that they may never be able to recover from the experience. Counselors who have experienced the Gestalt approach as a client can better assure their clients that this will not be the case. While the focus in counseling is on the present, rather than the past or the future, the Gestalt approach addresses both the past and future through experiencing emotions related to the past and future right now.

One goal of the Gestalt approach is to increase the client's level of self-awareness and her or his ability to accept responsibility for her or his choices. The counselor offers the client opportunities for self-expression (see **Techniques**). The client is encouraged to make statements about herself or himself rather than ask questions and to use "I" language. The Gestalt approach works especially well with groups.

Techniques

Before any activities are presented to the client, the client must have an effective relationship with the counselor. Additionally, the counselor must carefully consider the needs and goals of the client to select an appropriate activity. The client must also be willing to take the risk of fully experiencing her or his emotions.

Perhaps the most famous technique is the Empty Chair. A client is asked first to imagine a significant person (such as a parent or spouse) in an empty chair and then to have a "conversation" about an important unresolved event with that person. The counselor assists the client by encouraging the client to more fully experience her or his emotions, to truly share what is felt.

Clients may also be invited to act out what they feel they cannot do. For example, a client who feels she is a failure might be asked to experience the feeling of failure to excess. Processing with the client may help the client realize how successful she was in failing, and build from this foundation.

There are other classical Gestalt techniques. However, it is most important that the counselor use her or his creativity to develop specific activities for each client. The techniques of the Gestalt approach are less important than the counseling relationship.

Further Reading

Clarkson, P. (2000). *Gestalt counselling in action.* Thousand Oaks, CA: Sage Publications.

▼▼▼
Person-Centered Approach

The person-centered approach, also known as the Rogerian approach and humanism, brought sweeping changes to the practice of counseling. The person-centered approach is effective by itself and also works very well with most other counseling approaches.

Foundation

The focus of the person-centered approach is the relationship between client and counselor. This relationship is used to foster the client's growth. From Rogers's perspective, several conditions are needed to encourage the client to change. These conditions are Unconditional Positive Regard, Accurate Empathic Understanding, and Congruence (Corey, 1996). Unconditional Positive Regard occurs when the counselor values the client for who she or he is without any expectation that the client should be different from who she or he is. Accurate Empathic Understanding occurs when the counselor takes every opportunity to "walk in the client's shoes" and view the client's world as the client views it. Congruence occurs when the counselor is herself or himself during the session without hiding behind a role, such as that of a counselor.

These conditions—Unconditional Positive Regard, Accurate Empathic Understanding, and Congruence—form a uniquely human relationship between client and counselor. It is in this type of relationship that clients grow, change, and develop. In the absence of these conditions, change, according to Rogers, is not likely to occur.

Techniques

The person-centered approach does not rely on techniques; rather, it relies on the relationship between counselor and client to produce changes the client desires. Of course, the person-centered counselor needs skills. To be effective, the counselor needs excellent communication skills (chief among these are listening and a sense of adventure), a willingness to take a journey of discovery with the client, and an openness to sharing one's own experiences with the client through appropriate self-disclosure.

Further Reading

Kirshenbaum, H., & Henderson, V. L. (Eds.). (1989). *The Carl Rogers reader.* New York: Houghton Mifflin.
Rogers, C. R. (1961). *On becoming a person.* Boston: Houghton Mifflin.

Psychoanalytic Approach

Sigmund Freud developed the first—and by far the most comprehensive and misunderstood—theory of counseling and human development. Few other theories have had as profound an impact on our culture, thinking, and language as Freud's. His theory added numerous words and concepts to our language. Freudian terms in our daily lexicon include *defense mechanism, denial, ego, superego, id, conscious, unconscious, psychosexual development*—and the list goes on and on.

Foundation

Psychoanalytic theory is founded on the "holy trinity" of personality: id, ego, and superego. Hidden in the unconscious, the id is considered to be the most basic, instinctual part of the personality. The id seeks to fulfill its needs and wants immediately and is said to operate on the pleasure principle. Containing all the rules we learn as children, the superego helps regulate the id and ego. The part of our personality of which we are most aware is the ego. The ego strives to meet the needs of both the id and the superego and is said to operate on the reality principle (Corey, 1996).

Meeting the needs of both the id and superego often leads to anxiety. As a result, the ego develops defense mechanisms to protect itself from anxiety. Freudian defense mechanisms include projection, sublimation, regression, introjection, denial, rationalization, identification, compensation, repression, and reaction formation. Defense mechanisms by themselves are not a problem; however, their overapplication creates problems. The goals of strengthening the ego and making the unconscious conscious are met in part by addressing these defense mechanisms.

According to Freud, the personality develops in five stages and is fully developed by age 18. The five stages of personality development are oral, anal, phallic, latency, and genital. Development in each stage affects development in each successive stage. Developmental traumas cause unconscious fixations that impede not only future development, but also interpersonal relationships.

Techniques

Traditionally, the psychoanalytic counseling approach begins with free association. Interpretation, dream analysis, and analysis of resistance and transference all are used to resolve unconscious conflicts, improve insight, strengthen the ego, and develop awareness. Clients participate in counseling three to five times a week for several years. The counselor's role is to be a blank screen for the client's transferences and to ask guiding questions to help the client develop her or his own interpretations of her or his development.

The cost associated with the traditional psychoanalytic approach prohibits many clients from participating. However, portions of the psychoanalytic approach can be used with almost any client when combined with other approaches.

Further Reading

Freud, S. (1990). *The ego and the id: The standard edition of the complete psychological works of Sigmund Freud* (J. Strachey, Ed., & J. Riviere, Trans.). New York: Norton.

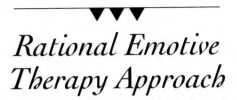

Rational Emotive
Therapy Approach

Also called RET or REBT (Rational Emotive Behavior Therapy), this highly effective approach was developed by Albert Ellis. Although RET is primarily a cognitive approach, it does not ignore feelings. RET is used to deal with a wide variety of challenges and is especially effective with clients who like to think about their problems.

Foundation

RET contends that changing thoughts will also change feelings and actions. Ellis states that thoughts are the easiest of the three elements to change, so the focus of counseling should be on cognitions. RET uses the ABCDEF approach: *A* represents Activating event. *B* represents our Beliefs about the activating event. *C* represents a Consequence of our beliefs—a feeling or an action. *D* represents Disputing thoughts—those thoughts that dispute our beliefs about the activating event. *E* represents the Effect of disputing thoughts, changes in feelings, and/or actions. *F* represents a change in Feeling about the activating event.

Our thoughts come in two varieties: rational and irrational. It is our irrational thoughts that cause problems in our lives. Using the ABCDEF approach, irrational thoughts are replaced with rational ones, producing healthier living. Irrational thoughts are often reflected in the client's language as *should's, must's, ought to's,* and so on.

Techniques

RET uses a variety of techniques that have at their core the goal of changing irrational thoughts into rational ones. This might include role-playing, guided imagery, eliminating negative words (*must, have to, should,* etc.), from the client's lexicon, actively disputing irrational thoughts, and creating homework assignments consisting of activities the client can do.

Further Reading

Blau, S., & Ellis, A. (Eds.). *The Albert Ellis reader: A guide to well-being using rational emotive behavior therapy.* New York: Citadel Press.

Reality Therapy Approach

William Glasser's reality therapy is a powerful approach for working with clients because most clients understand the approach easily and, in many circumstances, improvement can be seen and felt quickly.

Foundation

Glasser postulated four needs that guide and motivate behavior: belonging, power, freedom, and fun (Corey, 1996). According to Glasser, all behavior is designed to meet these needs. Behavior, which fails to meet these needs adequately, is a prime candidate for change. If what the client is doing is not working, it is time to try something else.

At the center of the reality approach is choice theory. Choice theory describes how a person's choices lead to some level of satisfaction of the four needs. The reality approach is desirable, in part, because it relies on the client's abilities and strengths to promote change. A total behavior is comprised of our thinking, feeling, doing, and physiology. Each total behavior helps the client obtain the four needs.

The counselor's goal is to help the client become more aware of her or his responsibility for making choices that affect her or his life. The counselor accomplishes this goal through teaching the client the core concepts of the reality approach and serves as a role model. The counselor works with the client in developing a specific plan for changing behavior.

Techniques

As is common in many counseling approaches, the relationship between counselor and client is important to the process of change. Clients need to feel cared for, understood, and respected before specific plans to change behavior can be created. Sessions focus on present experience and behavior and encourage the client to evaluate the effectiveness and appropriateness of her or his own choices. The counselor assists the client in developing a realistic plan for change based on the client's success identity and strengths.

Further Reading

Glasser, W. (1998). *Choice theory: A new psychology of personal freedom.* New York: HarperCollins.

Systems Approaches

All systems approaches seek to change the entire system through improved interactions within the system. Systems theory assumes that all elements of a system are interrelated. As a result, change to one component of the system will, in time, effect change in all parts of the system. Working within systems is exciting and challenging. It is exciting because the possibility exists that you will witness great change in the system. It is challenging because most systems resist change. Although systems approaches are most often used with families, they are not limited to families only. Systems approaches could also be used with businesses or other workgroups. From a systems point of view, each client is most fully understood within the context of the system.

Many theorists developed family systems approaches, including Minuchin, Haley, and Madanes; and Whitaker, Satir, and Bowen. Each of their approaches has a slightly different time focus, with different techniques, goals, and counselor roles. Many families who seek counseling desire help with a specific problem; as a result, a blending of solution-focused techniques (see **Brief/Solution-Focused Approach**) may be beneficial.

As an example, consider going to a cabin in the woods for a winter weekend getaway. When you arrive at the cabin, it is cold. After lighting the fireplace, you notice it is very warm next to the fire; gradually the entire cabin becomes comfortable. Working with systems is no different. After a careful analysis of the system, you may choose to implement change in one area (the parent's communication patterns), to create eventual change in another area (the children's expression of anger).

Working with family systems is different from individual and group counseling. Specialized training can increase your effectiveness in working with families.

Further Reading

Bauserman, J. M., & Rule, W. R. (1995). *A brief history of systems approaches in counseling and psychotherapy.* Lanaham, MD: University Press of America.

Micucci, J. A. (2000). *The adolescent in family therapy: Breaking the cycle of conflict and control.* New York: Guilford.

Notes

_____

_____

_____

_____

_____

_____

_____

_____

PART FOUR

▼▼▼

Useful Forms and Phone Numbers

Your agency may provide some of these forms. If they do not, or if you find the agency forms do not meet your needs, you may use these. Your supervisor should approve these forms *before* you use them. If you practice independently, seek legal counsel to determine if these forms are adequate for your needs. Forms in this section may be photocopied for use in your counseling practice.

CLIENT NAME:		CLIENT NUMBER:	

DATE	LENGTH	CASENOTES
/ /		

AFFECT:	

SUICIDAL? Y N N/A
IF YES, EXPLAIN:

HOMICIDAL? Y N N/A
IF YES, EXPLAIN:

REFERRALS:

NEXT APPOINTMENT
/ / AT   : AM PM

CONSENT FOR AUDIO/VIDEO TAPING

Client's Name: _____   File Number: _____

I authorize _____ (Counselor's name) to audiotape and/or videotape my counseling sessions. I understand the tapes will be used for supervision purposes only, will not be made a part of my file, and will be destroyed after being used in supervision.

I understand that other graduate counseling students and counselor educators will listen to or view the taped sessions. Although all of these people are sworn to confidentiality, my counselor cannot ensure that others will maintain confidentiality. My counselor will take appropriate measures to ensure that no one else will listen to or view the taped sessions.

I may revoke this Consent for Audio/Video Taping at any time by submitting a written request to my counselor.

_____   ____/____/____
Client   Date

_____   ____/____/____
Counselor   Date

CONSENT FOR COMMUNICATION

I, _____, am currently consulting with:

	PROFESSIONAL	NAME	PHONE NUMBER
_____	Counselor	_____	( ) _____
_____	Psychologist	_____	( ) _____
_____	Psychiatrist	_____	( ) _____
_____	Family Physician	_____	( ) _____
_____	School Counselor	_____	( ) _____
_____	Pastoral Counselor	_____	( ) _____
_____	Other ( )	_____	( ) _____

I, _____ (Client's Name), release my counselor, _____

(Counselor's Name), to contact the above professionals from whom I am currently receiving services.

_____   ____/____/____
Client   Date

_____   ____/____/____
Counselor   Date

DISCLOSURE STATEMENT

All counselors need a disclosure statement. Your disclosure statement tells your clients what they can expect from you and about your training and experiences. Writing a disclosure statement takes time, because at the core of your disclosure statement are your beliefs about counseling and about human nature.

Typically, disclosure statements include information about:

- Your status as an intern or licensed professional
- Your education and training
- What to do in an emergency
- Whom to contact with complaints

- Who will supervise you
- Confidentiality
- What is in the client's file
- The client's rights

- Your approach to counseling
- Fees
- Making and changing appointments

Your school, agency, or state licensing authority may require you to include additional information in your disclosure statement. You may want to consider having Braille, audio, and/or non-English versions of your disclosure statement produced.

For every client you counsel, give the client a copy of your disclosure statement and place a copy of it in the client's file.

A sample disclosure statement, formatted as a tri-fold brochure, is included to help you get started.

For an expanded discussion of disclosure statements, see:

Keel, L. P., & Brown, S. P. (1999, July). Professional Disclosure Statements. *Counseling Today,* pp. 14, 33.

This disclosure statement is provided to inform you of my approach to counseling. If you have questions about the information in this brochure, please ask me at any time.

COUNSELING AS A PROCESS

Counseling with me begins with a relationship and involves active work in an ongoing process. We will explore your present situation, the changes you would like to see happen, what these changes look like, your needs and wants, your safety, and your emotions. I approach counseling with an accepting, egalitarian, multicultural approach. As your counselor, I will support and challenge you. The process of change is hard work and I encourage you to keep working even when it's difficult.

LENGTH OF COUNSELING

Counseling sessions are normally 50 minutes and begin on the hour. Financial matters are made in accordance with this agency and not with me. The number and frequency of sessions depends on your needs. Please leave your pager and/or cell phone in your car.

QUALIFICATIONS

• **Temporary LPC # 887766**
• **Master of Arts** in Community Counseling from Southwest University.
• **Bachelor of Science** in Humanities from Western University.

COUNSELING EXPERIENCE

• LMNOP Counseling, Inc.

Conversations between client and counselor are confidential as governed by the laws of this state. What you tell me stays between you and me and me and my supervisor with five exceptions:

• If you threaten to harm yourself or another person.
• If you report the abuse of a child.
• If you report the abuse of an elderly person.
• If you report sexual exploitation by a counselor, therapist, or other mental health professional.
• State law mandates that mental health professionals may need to report these situations to the appropriate persons and/or agencies.

• Your counseling records may be subpoenaed by a state or federal court of law if legal action is taken against you.

Except in the circumstances described above, I will not release any information about you to any person or agency without your prior, written consent.

Note: If you are under the age of 18 your parent or guardian has a legal right to access your file.

TO THOSE CURRENTLY IN COUNSELING

If you are currently receiving counseling services from a counselor, psychologist, or psychiatrist I may not be able to offer you services. If this is the case, I will discuss your options for mental health care with you.

All mental health counselors keep records of their counseling sessions. Your file contains the initial paperwork you completed for this agency, my intake completed during our first session, your signed Limits of Confidentiality form, my case notes and treatment plan, copies of all referrals I make, copies of all homework assignments you complete, copies of all handouts I give you, and any materials from other counselors you have seen at this agency. Your file contains detailed information about you. I am happy to review your file with you at any time. If you would like to review your file please ask me to schedule an appointment with you for this purpose.

REFERRAL TO OTHER AGENCIES

From time to time I may refer you to other agencies for services. Some of the circumstances in which I may refer you include if you request or require medical care, if you have questions best answered by an attorney, or if your counseling needs are not addressed by this agency. I will discuss any referral I make with you.

EMERGENCIES

If you feel you are a danger to yourself or to someone else you are encouraged to contact the nearest hospital emergency room. You may ask how you can reach me for emergencies.

SU Counseling Center

- LMNOP Counseling, Inc.

Sample

Sample

Disclosure
Statement

CHRIS COUNSELOR, M.A.
LPC Intern

EXCUSE FROM WORK OR SCHOOL

COUNSELOR'S NAME, AGENCY NAME, ADDRESS, AND PHONE NUMBER:

To Whom It May Concern: Our File #: _____

____ Please excuse _____ from work/school today.

_____ had an appointment in my office to discuss personal concerns.

____ Please excuse _____ from work/school from ____/____/____ to ____/____/____.

Notes:

_____

_____

_____   ____/____/____
Counselor's Signature   Date

CONFIDENTIAL

INTAKE

Date: ____/____/____   Client #: _____

PERSONAL INFORMATION

Name: _____

Address: _____

City: _____ State: ____ Zip Code: _____

County: _____

Day phone: ( ) _____

Okay to leave messages?   ❏ Yes ❏ No

US Citizen?   ❏ Yes   ❏ No

If no, immigration status: _____

Date of Birth: ____/____/____ Age: _____

Sex: ❏ Female   ❏ Male   ❏ Unknown

Night phone: ( ) _____

Okay to leave messages?   ❏ Yes ❏ No

SEXUAL ORIENTATION	ETHNICITY	LEVEL OF EDUCATION
Heterosexual	❏ American Indian or Alaskan Native	❏ None
Gay	❏ Asian American	❏ Elementary School
Lesbian	❏ Black/African American	❏ Middle School
Bisexual	❏ Hispanic	❏ High School
Transgendered	❏ Multiracial	❏ GED
Other	❏ Pacific Islander	❏ Vocational Training
Unknown	❏ White	❏ Some College
	❏ Other	❏ College Degree
	❏ Unknown	❏ Graduate/Professional School

RELATIONSHIP STATUS		RELATIONSHIP HISTORY
Legally Married	Length:_____	_____
Common Law Marriage	Length:_____	_____
Legally Divorced	Length:_____	_____
Separated	Length:_____	_____
Life Partner	Length:_____	_____
Dating	Length:_____	_____
Living Together	Length:_____	_____
Single		_____

Who does the client live with? _____

_____

_____

Children's names and ages:

_____ _____

_____ _____

_____ _____

GENOGRAM

PRESENTING PROBLEM OR CONCERN:

_____
_____
_____
_____

CURRENT EMPLOYMENT	CURRENTLY ON PROBATION/PAROLE
Where:_____	❑ Yes. Officer: _____
Position:_____	Charged with: _____
If unemployed, why? _____	

COUNSELING HISTORY	FAMILY HISTORY OF COUNSELING
Previous history of mental health/pastoral counseling?	Family history of counseling? ❑ Yes ❑ No
❑ Yes ❑ No If yes, details: When ___/___	If yes, details: When ___/___
Counselor: _____	Counselor: _____
Treated for: _____	Treated for: _____
_____	_____

PENDING COURT CASE	SUBSTANCE USE
❑ Yes ❑ No Details: _____	❑ Caffeine Frequency: _____
_____	❑ Tobacco Frequency: _____
_____	❑ Alcohol Frequency: _____
_____	❑ Drugs: Frequency: _____
_____	Other details: _____
_____	_____
_____	_____
Recovering alcoholic? ❑ Yes ❑ No	Family history of alcoholism? ❑ Yes ❑ No
Recovering drug addict? ❑ Yes ❑ No	Family history of drug abuse? ❑ Yes ❑ No
Previous treatment for drug/alcohol abuse?	Needle use? ❑ Yes ❑ No
❑ Yes ❑ No If yes, details: When ___/___	HIV test? ❑ Yes ❑ No
Treatment facility: _____	Date: ___/___ Result: _____
_____	Hepatitis test? ❑ Yes ❑ No
Other Information:_____	Date: ___/___ Result: _____
_____	
_____	

MEDICAL HISTORY	
Current medical treatment? ❑ Yes ❑ No	Doctor's name and address:
If yes, details: _____	_____
_____	_____
_____	_____
_____	( )_____-_____
Physical conditions/diagnoses: _____	Current medications & dosages: _____
_____	_____
_____	_____
_____	_____

ast medications for mental disorders: _____

_____

_____

hildhood illnesses and injuries: _____

_____

_____

_____

Head injuries: _____

_____

_____

Hospitalizations: _____

_____

_____

_____

AFFECT

Flat ❑ Sad ❑ Happy ❑ Expansive ❑ Angry

Confused ❑ Nervous ❑ Inappropriate

Other: _____

OBSERVED BEHAVIORS

_____

_____

_____

ABUSIVE EXPERIENCES

Client reported being sexually abused as a child.

_____

_____

_____

_____

_____

❑ Client's parents were abusive to each other.

❑ Client's parents were abusive to their children.

❑ Client's siblings were abusive to each other.

❑ Client's siblings were abusive to their parents.

❑ Client reports currently being abusive.

❑ Client reports currently being abused.

SEXUAL HISTORY

_____

_____

_____

_____

_____

OTHER

_____

_____

_____

_____

CURRENT ABUSE

Most recent incident: _____

_____

_____

Worst incident: _____

_____

_____

First incident: _____

_____

_____

_____

SUICIDAL IDEATION

urrent suicidal thoughts/attempts ❑ Yes ❑ No

ast suicidal thoughts/attempts ❑ Yes ❑ No

etails: _____

HOMICIDAL IDEATION

Current homicidal thoughts/attempts ❑ Yes ❑ No

Past homicidal thoughts/attempts ❑ Yes ❑ No

Details: _____

_____

GOALS

1. _____
   _____

2. _____
   _____

3. _____
   _____

4. _____
   _____

How will you know when these goals have bee[n] reached? _____
_____
_____
_____
_____
_____
_____
_____
_____

CLINICAL IMPRESSIONS/OBSERVATIONS	MULTI-AXIAL DIAGNOSIS
_____	AXIS I: _____
_____	AXIS II: _____
_____	AXIS III: _____
_____	AXIS IV: _____
_____	AXIS V: _____

PREFERRED APPOINTMENT TIME

S   M   T   W   T   F   S   AM/PM

❑ Gave client a copy of my disclosure statement

❑ Language Needs:

COUNSELOR SIGNATURE

RELIGIOUS PREFERENCE

❑ Buddhist   ❑ Catholic   ❑ Jewish   ❑ Muslim

❑ Non-denominational ❑ Protestant

❑ Born-again Christian ❑ Other ❑ None

Date: /   /

❑ Client deemed inappropriate for this facility [or] agency. Referred to:

INTERNSHIP LOG

Internship Site:	Intern's Name:
From: / / To: / /	Supervisor's Signature:

DATE	ACTIVITY	TIME

SUMMARY

INDIVIDUAL COUNSELING:	GROUP COUNSELING:	FAMILY COUNSELING:	CRISIS COUNSELING:
ACADEMIC COUNSELING:	CAREER COUNSELING:	SUBSTANCE ABUSE COUNSELING:	SUPERVISION:
PASTORAL COUNSELING:	CHARTING:	CONSULTATION:	OTHER:

Client Name: _____   Client #: _____

Information discussed in the counseling setting is held confidential and will not be shared without the written permission of the client except under the following conditions:

- The client threatens to harm self or another person.

- The client reports the abuse of a child, a person who is elderly, or a person who is disabled.

- The client reports sexual exploitation by a counselor, therapist, or other mental health professional.

- Your counseling records may be subpoenaed by a state or federal court of law if legal action is taken against you.

I agree to these limits of confidentiality.

_____ ____/____/____   _____ ____/____/____
Client's Signature   Date   Parent or Guardian's Signature   Date

_____ ____/____/____
Counselor's Signature   Date

LIMITS OF CONFIDENTIALITY
FOR GROUP COUNSELING

Client Name: _____   Client #: _____

Confidentiality is a cornerstone of effective group counseling. Confidentiality is important because it helps people in the group feel safe. This safe feeling invites members to participate, and participation is the key to change. Confidentiality requires the help of everyone in the group.

As your counselor, I will not share any information about you with anyone outside this agency without your prior written consent, with the exception of these situations:

- If you threaten to harm yourself or another person.
- If you report the abuse of a child, a person who is elderly, or a person who is disabled.
- If you report sexual exploitation by another mental health professional.
- Your counseling records may be subpoenaed by a state or federal court of law if legal action is taken against you.

Note: If you are mandated by another agency to attend this group, regular communications about your progress will be made to that agency.

Note: If you are a minor, your parent or guardian has a legal right to access your file.

I will revisit the topic of confidentiality periodically during the group.

While I will not violate your confidentiality, I cannot guarantee that other members of this group will protect your confidentiality. Any breech of confidentiality must be discussed with the group as soon as possible after it occurs. The best way to avoid violating another group member's confidentiality is only to talk about yourself if someone asks you about your counseling. If you keep a journal or diary, it is critical that you write only about your own experiences in it and that no one else has access to it.

All questions about confidentiality should be asked in the group.

I agree to these limits of confidentiality.

_____   ____/____/____
Client's Signature   Date

_____   ____/____/____
Counselor's Signature   Date

NO-SUICIDE CONTRACT

Client Name: _____   Client #: _____

- • I will not hurt myself.

- • I will not attempt to hurt myself.

- • I will not kill myself.

- • I will call 911 if I cannot keep these promises.

- • My next appointment is on _____ at _____.

_____   ____/____/____
Client's Signature   Date

_____   ____/____/____
Counselor's Signature   Date

Adapted from Getz, W. L., Allen, D. B., Myers, R. K., & Lindner, K. C. (1983). *Brief counseling with suicida persons.* Lexington, MA: D. C. Heath.

Counselor: Keep a copy of this form for the client's file and provide the client with a copy to take home.

REFERRAL FOR SERVICES

COUNSELOR'S NAME, AGENCY NAME, ADDRESS, AND PHONE NUMBER:

_____ is referred to: Our File #: _____

                    _____
                    _____
                    _____
                    (_____)_____

                    for these services:

_____ Evaluation for possible medication for
        anxiety/depression/insomnia/migraine headache

_____ Physical exam—client reports these physical complaints:

        _____
        _____
        _____

_____ Treatment for alcoholism/drug addiction

_____ Mental health counseling
        Primary concern: _____

_____ Evaluation of suicidality

_____ To apply for a protective order

_____ HIV testing & counseling

_____ Other: _____

_____ Please send a copy of your findings to me at the address above.

_____   ____/____/____
Counselor's Signature   Date

I, _____ (Client's Name), authorize and request that _____ (Counselor's Name) release all confidential information in my file to:

_____

_____

_____

_____

(   )_____

I understand that I may revoke this consent at any time by submitting a written request to my counselor. I release my counselor and her or his agency from all legal liability for the release of this information. This form expires one year from the date below.

_____   ____/____/____
Client's Signature   Date

_____   ____/____/____
Counselor's Signature   Date

REPORT OF INFORMATION

COUNSELOR'S NAME, AGENCY NAME, ADDRESS, AND PHONE NUMBER:

CLIENT NAME	CLIENT FILE NUMBER

DATE OF CLIENT DISCLOSURE	DATE OF REPORT	TIME OF REPORT
/ /	/ /	AM / PM

NAME OF THE AGENCY CALLED	PHONE NUMBER CALLED
	( )

NAME OF THE PERSON SPOKEN WITH FROM THE AGENCY	❑ MARK THIS BOX IF YOU GAVE THE AGENCY YOUR NAME AND AGENCY AFFILIATION WHEN YOU CALLED.

DETAILED DESCRIPTION OF THE REPORT I MADE

COUNSELOR SIGNATURE	SUPERVISOR SIGNATURE
Date: / /	Date: / /

SUICIDE ASSESSMENT CHECKLIST

This form is intended to be used to guide and document comprehensive risk assessment. It should be used conjunction with other interview and historical data as an aid in determining appropriate client disposition. It is ne intended as a predictive device and should not be used as such. However, the higher the scores, the mor concern one should have regarding potential suicidal behaviors.

CLIENT'S NAME _____ AGE _____ SEX   MALE   FEMALE

PART 1

ASSESSING SUICIDAL RISK: Circle all of the items relating to the client's situation and sum the correspondin scores at the end of PART 1.

CLIENT HAS A DEFINITE PLAN: YES (6)   PREVIOUS PSYCHIATRIC HISTORY: YES (

METHOD:	FIREARM (10)	CAR EXHAUST (7)	HANGING (9)
	DROWNING (6)	SUFFOCATING (6)	JUMPING (5)
	DRUGS/POISON (6)	CUTTING (3)	OTHER (3): _____

METHOD ON HAND:	YES (5)	SUICIDE SURVIVOR:	YES (6)
MAKING FINAL PLANS:	YES (6)	DRUG AND/OR ALCOHOL USE:	YES (5)
PRIOR ATTEMPT(S):	YES (5)	MALE 15-35 OR 65 AND OLDER:	YES (5)
SUICIDE NOTE:	YES (6)	DEPENDENT CHILDREN AT HOME:	YES (-4)

MARITAL STATUS: SINGLE (3) MARRIED (2) DIVORCED (5) SEPARATED (5) WIDOWED (5)

PART 2

From your interview, rate your impression of the client's status on each of the following items. Ratings should b based on *initial perceptions* of the client's status rather than on changes resulting from any intervention. Sum th corresponding item ratings at the end of PART 2 (minimum score = 9).

	NONE				EXTREME
SENSE OF HOPELESSNESS:	1	2	3	4	5
SENSE OF WORTHLESSNESS:	1	2	3	4	5
SOCIAL ISOLATION:	1	2	3	4	5
DEPRESSION:	1	2	3	4	5
IMPULSIVITY:	1	2	3	4	5
HOSTILITY:	1	2	3	4	5
INTENT TO DIE:	1	2	3	4	5
ENVIRONMENTAL STRESS:	1	2	3	4	5
FUTURE TIME PERSPECTIVE:	1	2	3	4	5

The level of stress precipitated by any actual or anticipated events in the client's life, such as loss of a loved one, change in life style, humiliation, etc.

PART 2 TOTAL: _____
PART 1 TOTAL: _____
TOTAL SCORE: _____ (Sum of PART 1 + PART 2)

Was the client engaged in a "no suicide" contract?   YES   NO   NOT APPROPRIATE
Considering all of the information available, indicate the client's level of suicide risk on the following scale:
LOW RISK   1   2   3   4   5   HIGH RISK

Disposition of referral: _____

COUNSELOR'S SIGNATURE: _____ DATE: _____

SUICIDE ASSESSMENT CHECKLIST TERMINOLOGY SHEET

following are brief definitions or explanations of the terms used in the Suicide Assessment Checklist.

PART 1

ENT HAS A DEFINITE PLAN—Has the client formulated a plan to commit suicide other than a vague "I'm going ill myself?"

THOD—If the client does have a concrete plan, which method has she/he chosen?

THOD ON HAND—Is the method one that is readily available to the client as opposed to one that needs to be ained?

EVIOUS PSYCHIATRIC HISTORY—Psychiatric history is used here as a broad term to include the range from atient psychiatric care to outpatient psychotherapy.

KING FINAL PLANS—Is the client taking care of "unfinished business" and/or giving away prized possessions?

IOR ATTEMPT(S)—Has the client admitted to previously attempted suicide or described situations that may ve been "hidden" attempts?

ICIDE NOTE—Has the client written or is he/she planning to write a suicide note placing blame for the action, ving instructions to survivors, or saying "goodbye"?

ICIDE SURVIVOR—Has the client had a close friend or relative who has committed suicide?

RUG/ALCOHOL USE—Does the client use alcohol or drugs at any level?

ALE 15–35 OR 65 AND OLDER—Is the client a male in either of these age categories?

EPENDENT CHILDREN AT HOME—Does the client have one or more children 18 years or younger living in the usehold?

ARITAL STATUS—What is the marital status of the client?

Ratings of the following items are to be based upon your impressions of the client's status or "feelings." For example, how hopeless does the client "seem" to feel as opposed to how hopeless you think the client "should" feel based upon initial impressions of the client's status rather than on the client's feelings resulting from success resolution of the presenting situations.

SENSE OF HOPELESSNESS—To what degree does the client "feel" that there is no hope of improvement in his/her situation in the future?

SENSE OF WORTHLESSNESS—To what degree does the client "feel" that she/he has no personal worth or val to him/herself and others?

SOCIAL ISOLATION—To what degree does the client "feel" that she/he has no friends and relatives to whom he/she can turn?

DEPRESSION—To what degree does the client exhibit signs of depression, i.e., inactivity, lack of interest, disrupted eating and/or sleeping habits, etc.?

IMPULSIVITY—To what degree does the client exhibit impulsive behavior, i.e., acting with little rational thought to outcomes?

HOSTILITY—How much anger does the client seem to have towards him or herself or others, or institutions?

INTENT TO DIE—To what degree does the client seem determined to carry out his/her plan to their conclusion?

ENVIRONMENTAL STRESS—To what degree does the client "feel" that events in his/her life are "overwhelming," painful, humiliating or are providing insurmountable obstacles?

FUTURE TIME PERSPECTIVE—To what extent is the client able to focus on the future or positive future events as opposed to focusing on only the present or negative events? This item is scored in the opposite direction from the previous Part 2 items. That is, the absence of positive future time perspective is scored 5.

TERMINATION SUMMARY

Client Name: _____ File #: _____ Date: / /

PRESENTING PROBLEM OR CONCERN:

_____
_____
_____
_____

CLINICAL IMPRESSIONS/OBSERVATIONS	MULTI-AXIAL DIAGNOSIS
_____	AXIS I: _____
_____	AXIS II: _____
_____	AXIS III: _____
_____	AXIS IV: _____
_____	AXIS V: _____

GOALS	INTERVENTION
_____	1. _____
_____	2. _____
_____	3. _____
_____	4. _____

PROGRESS	REASON FOR TERMINATION
_____	_____
_____	_____
_____	_____
_____	_____

COUNSELOR SIGNATURE

Date: / /

SUMMARY

# of Sessions	Type
	Individual
	Group
	Couple/Family

TREATMENT PLAN

Client Name: _____ File #: _____ Date: / /

PRESENTING PROBLEM OR CONCERN:

_____
_____
_____
_____

CLINICAL IMPRESSIONS/OBSERVATIONS	MULTI-AXIAL DIAGNOSIS AT TERMINATION
_____	Axis I: _____
_____	Axis II: _____
_____	Axis III: _____
_____	Axis IV: _____
_____	Axis V: _____

GOALS	INTERVENTION
1. _____	1. _____
2. _____	2. _____
3. _____	3. _____
4. _____	4. _____

CLIENT'S SIGNATURE	COUNSELOR'S SIGNATURE
Date: / /	Date: / /

REVIEW

DATE	PROGRESS	ATTAINED GOALS
/ /		❏ 1 ❏ 2 ❏ 3 ❏ 4
/ /		❏ 1 ❏ 2 ❏ 3 ❏ 4
/ /		❏ 1 ❏ 2 ❏ 3 ❏ 4
/ /		❏ 1 ❏ 2 ❏ 3 ❏ 4

FREQUENTLY CALLED NUMBERS

Using your local telephone directory, record phone numbers for these services here ⟶

Alcoholics Anonymous ....

Area Agency on Aging ....

Battered Women's Shelter ....

Child Protective Services ....

Children's Shelter ....

Consumer Credit Counseling ....

Crisis Pregnancy Center ....

Dental Clinic ....

Detoxification Services ....

Equal Employment Opportunity Commission ....

Gamblers Anonymous ....

Hospice ....

HIV Testing ....

Hospital ....

Legal Aid ....

Medical Clinic ....

Narcotics Anonymous ....

Parenting Classes ....

Poison Control Center ....

Police Department (non-emergency number) ....

Protective Orders ....

Rape Crisis Center ....

Salvation Army ....

Social Services ....

State Unemployment Benefits ....

Suicide Prevention ....

United Way ....

Veteran's Administration Hospital ....

Use this space to record other frequently called numbers:

....

....

....

....

....

....

NATIONAL HOTLINE NUMBERS

AIDS/HIV Information...800-342-243
Alcohol Information 800-729-668
Domestic Violence 800-799-723
Federal Bureau of Investigation 888-225-532
Hepatitis Information 888-443-723
Mental Health Information..800-789-264
Missing & Exploited Children 800-843-567
National Youth Crisis Hotline 800-448-466
Poison Control 800-764-766
Runaway..800-621-400

Use this space to record other hotline numbers:

....
....
....
....
....
....
....
....
....
....
....
....
....
....
....
....
....
....

References

Ackroyd, E. (1993). *A Dictionary of Dream Symbols: With an Introduction to Dream Psychology.* New York: Sterling Publishing Co., Inc.

American Psychiatric Association. (2000). *Diagnostic and Statistical Manual of Mental Disorders* (4th ed., text revised). Washington, DC: Author.

Corey, G. (1996). *Theory and Practice of Counseling and Psychotherapy* (5th ed.). Pacific Grove, CA: Brooks/Cole, Inc.

Getz, W. L., Allen, D. B., Myers, R. K., & Lindner, K. C. (1983). *Brief counseling with suicidal persons.* Lexington, MA: D. C. Heath.

Haugaard, J. J., & Repucci, N. D. (1988). *The Sexual Abuse of Children: A Comprehensive Guide to Current Knowledge and Intervention Strategies.* San Francisco, CA: Jossey-Bass, Inc.

Kalichman, S. C. (1996). *Answering Your Questions About AIDS.* Washington, DC: American Psychological Association.

Keel, L. P., & Brown, S. P. (1999, July). Professional Disclosure Statements. *Counseling Today,* pp. 14, 33.

Konopasek, D. E. (2000). *Medication "Fact Sheets."* Anchorage, Alaska: Arctic Tern Publishing Co.

Leman, K. (1998). *The New Birth Order Book: Why You Are the Way You Are.* Grand Rapids, MI: Revell Publishing Co.

McGoldrick, M, & Gerson, R. (1985). *Genograms in Family Assessment.* New York: W. W. Norton & Co.

Prochaska, J. O., & Norcross, J. C. (1994). *Systems of Psychotherapy: A Transtheoretical Analysis* (3rd ed.). Pacific Grove, CA: Brooks/Cole, Inc.

Rogers, J. R., Alexander, R. A., Subich, L. M. (1994). Development and Psychometric Analysis of the Suicide Assessment Checklist. *Journal of Mental Health Counseling,* 16 (3), 352–368.

Santrock, J. W. (1995). *Life-span Development* (5th ed.) Madison, WI: WCB, Brown & Benchmark Publishers.

Telep, V. *Secrets Can Hurt: Some Facts About Sexual Abuse.* Virginia Department of Social Services.

Index

TO THE READER

want to hear from you! How could I make this book more helpful to you? What did you like about this book? What's missing? I'll use your thoughts, suggestions, and comments to improve the next edition. If you would prefer you may contact me by e-mail (ptravers@stic.net) or write to me in care of Brooks/Cole at 511 Forest Lodge Road, Pacific Grove, CA 93950.

How would you describe your practice setting?

❑ Non-profit community agency   ❑ College counseling center   ❑ Elementary school   ❑ Middle school   ❑ Hospital

❑ High school   ❑ Private practice

❑ Children's advocacy center   ❑ Retirement community   ❑ Child protective services   ❑ Rape crisis center   ❑ Career counseling center

❑ Other: _____

I am a:

❑ Counselor   ❑ Counselor intern   ❑ Counselor educator   ❑ Social worker

❑ Case worker   ❑ Psychologist   ❑ Graduate student   ❑ Other: _____

❑ I am currently in school. The name of the school is _____

The name of the program I am in is _____

This is a ❑ graduate program or an ❑ undergraduate program.

What I like best about this book is _____

_____

What I like least about this book is _____

_____

I wish this book had more information about _____

_____

❑ I am using this book to help me prepare for a state or national licensure examination.

Other comments I'd like to share: _____

_____

_____

_____

_____

_____

_____

Thank you!